Immigrants from
Great Britain and Ireland

"Immigrants from Great Britain and Ireland"

A Guide to Archival and Manuscript Sources in North America

compiled by
JACK W. WEAVER and DEEGEE LESTER

Reference Guides to Archives and Manuscript Collections
on Immigrant Culture, Number 1

GREENWOOD PRESS
Westport, Connecticut • London, England

Library of Congress Cataloging-in-Publication Data

Weaver, Jack W.
  Immigrants from Great Britain and Ireland.

  (Reference guides to archives and manuscript
collections on immigrant culture, ISSN 0885-7555 ; no. 1)
  Includes index.
    1. British Americans—History—Archival resources—
North America—Directories.   2. British—Canada—
History—Archival resources—North America—Directories.
3. Irish Americans—History—Archival resources—North
America—Directories.   4. Irish—Canada—History—
Archival resources—North America—Directories.
5. United States—Emigration and immigration—
Archival resources—North America—Directories.
6. Canada—Emigration and immigration—Archival
resources—North America—Directories.   I. Lester,
DeeGee.   II. Title.   III. Series.
Z1361.B74W43   1986   016.973'042   85-27325
[E184.B7]
ISBN 0-313-24342-5 (lib. bdg. : alk. paper)

REF
E
184
.B7
Cap. 1

Library of Congress Catalog Card Number: 85-27325
ISBN: 0-313-24342-5
ISSN: 0885-7555

First published in 1986

Greenwood Press
A division of Congressional Information Service, Inc.
88 Post Road West, Westport, Connecticut 06881

Printed in the United States of America

The paper used in this book complies with the
Permanent Paper Standard issued by the National
Information Standards Organization (Z39.48-1984).

10 9 8 7 6 5 4 3 2 1

CONTENTS

INTRODUCTION

Some time ago, with the blessing of the American Committee for Irish Studies, Michael J. Durkan (Librarian, Swarthmore College) and Maureen Murphy (Dean, Hofstra) began the process of collecting materials for an "Irish Resources Directory." In Tennessee, at or near the same time, DeeGee Lester was compiling lists and sending out questionnaires for a similar project. In South Carolina, Jack Wayne Weaver outlined still another project, persuaded Greenwood Press to consider it for publication, and began to collect his list of names and addresses and to prepare a questionnaire. At this point, Weaver and Lester discovered each other and agreed to collaborate. In an act of unparalleled generosity, Durkan and Murphy shared materials with the present collaborators and decided to postpone their own volume. Lester's compilations included published and unpublished materials in collections covering Irish literature and history, as well as genealogy/immigration collections in North America, Ireland, and Great Britain. Through the guidance of Mary Sive, Acquisitions Editor at Greenwood Press, Lester's compilations were divided. The unpublished immigration collections lists for North America were sent to Weaver and are included in this volume. The remaining materials covering resource collections in Irish history and literature will appear in a companion volume, entitled IRISH RESEARCH: A GUIDE TO COLLECTIONS IN NORTH AMERICA, IRELAND, AND GREAT BRITAIN, by Lester alone.

In order to make a comprehensive study of immigration in North America, the continent must be considered as a single entity. The purpose of this directory is to provide a view of immigration from this perspective. To a degree not adequately recognized, migration and emigration occurred between the Canadian and American territories and the subsequent nations. While the thirteen American colonies struggled to survive along the Atlantic seacoast, Scots traders and trappers, in Canada, vied with the French in dealing with the Indians. English settlers followed the Scottish traders; as in the American colonies, they brought their families and developed farms and towns. Irish and Welsh joined the English and Scots, in appreciable numbers, in both countries in the eighteenth century. At various times,

some immigrants in Canada moved south into what was to
become the United States, and some "Americans" moved north
into Canada. To cite only one example, American Colonial
Loyalists, during and after the American Revolutionary War,
fled the colonies in such numbers that, even today, some
villagers in Nova Scotia remember their ancestors came from
Virginia, Georgia, and the two Carolinas. There are published
studies for each ethnic group. For the Irish, see the several
works of Michael J. O'Brien, especially the IRISH IN AMERICA;
for the Scotch-Irish, Robert J. Dickson's ULSTER EMIGRATION
TO COLONIAL AMERICA 1718-1775; for the Scots, David Dobson's
DIRECTORY OF SCOTS BANISHED TO THE AMERICAN PLANTATION and
J.P. MacLean's HISTORICAL ACCOUNT OF THE SETTLEMENT OF SCOTCH
HIGHLANDERS IN AMERICA PRIOR TO THE PEACE OF 1783; for the
English, Jack and Marion Kaminkow's LIST OF EMIGRANTS FROM
ENGLAND TO AMERICA: and for the Welsh, Edward G. Hartmann's
AMERICANS FROM WALES. Seamus P. Metress connects Irish and
Scotch-Irish in THE IRISH-AMERICAN EXPERIENCE: A GUIDE TO
THE LITERATURE, as does Jack Wayne Weaver in SELECTED
PROCEEDINGS OF THE SCOTCH-IRISH HERITAGE FESTIVAL AT WINTHROP
COLLEGE IN 1980 and SELECTED PROCEEDINGS OF SCOTCH-IRISH
HERITAGE FESTIVAL II. For the field as a whole, Maxine Alcorn's
PASSENGERS AND IMMIGRANTS TO AMERICA: A BIBLIOGRAPHY (Clayton
Library, University of Houston) is a useful tool. One can
also benefit from reading of the numerous state and local
histories of the United States and of the provinces and
nation of Canada, and of the histories of various churches.

For unpublished or manuscript materials, some subject
guides already exist, but are often either general or dated.
These include Philip Hamer's GUIDE TO ARCHIVES AND MANU-
SCRIPTS IN THE U.S., the AMERICAN LIBRARY DIRECTORY, THE
DIRECTORY OF ARCHIVES AND MANUSCRIPT REPOSITORIES (National
Historical Publications and Records Commission), THE
OFFICIAL MUSEUM DIRECTORY, the Library of Congress's
NATIONAL UNION CATALOGUE OF MANUSCRIPT COLLECTIONS, and
others. This volume is, however, the first to focus exclusively on the English, Scots, Irish, and Welsh; groups which
furnished over fifty percent of the white settlers during
the seventeenth century and nearly sixty-six percent during
the eighteenth century. It has benefitted from the example
of the guides mentioned above and from the DIRECTORY OF
CANADIAN RECORDS AND MANUSCRIPT REPOSITORIES.

All books are collaborations of authors and perceptive
editors. This volume is no exception. Without the encourage-
ment of Mary Sive, it would not have existed. Without the
advice and example of W. Ronald Chepesiuk, Series Advisor,
it would have been in a different and less coherent form.
This volume and its compilers, however, owe additonal debts.
The compilers are also grateful to the librarians and
archivists in the United States and Canada. Without their
tireless efforts, there would have been little to write
about; without their help, we would have been unable to do
the writing. With deepest affection, we dedicate this directory
to them.

Jack Wayne Weaver   DeeGee Lester

METHODOLOGY

Compilers always hope to have an exhaustive annotated bibliography, but out of necessity, settle for one which is representative. Weaver and Lester began this bibliography with lists compiled from experience as Irish specialists, and Weaver added an additional specialty in the Scotch-Irish references. These lists were checked against similar lists in the directories mentioned in the introduction and were added to from suggestions made in replies to the initial questionnaires. Of the 1000 queries Weaver sent in his first mailing, he received 400 replies. These contained an additional 65 recommended sources, which were then queried. Many of the 400 replies had to be questioned a second time by means of letter or phone. For the 600 not replying, Weaver ran a second check using one of the many directories listed in the introduction to gauge the size and importance of the collections. Lester furnished materials for some of these as well. However, for some repositories, it was necessary to rely upon other directories, either to substitute for entries we could not write or to flesh out some skimpy responces that were received. In all cases, these are in parenthases. We are indebted completely to other directories for 92 of the total 389 entries, and this fact is signaled by listing the sources first, and then including the commentary within parentheses. When our own entries have been used as reference to others, we signal this fact by giving our annotation first and listing other sources last and parenthetically in "See Also" references. In this, we follow the example of the DIRECTORY OF ARCHIVES AND MANUSCRIPT REPOSITORIES (National Historical Publications and Records Commission).

In our directory, we have included the best sources and, where possible, some for each state, possession, and province. The original thirteen states, being the oldest, have more repositories than later states. Each village library often has some original materials, as does each historical and genealogical society, in those states. The later states, Michigan, Alabama, Texas, Utah, Arizona, and California, have amassed numerous outstanding collections. In Canada, the early provinces of Ontario, Newfoundland, New Brunswick, and Nova Scotia have the most important collections of materials related to our topic. Quebec, which also has sizable collections, has focused almost exclusively on its French cultural materials. For information on Quebec and later provinces, the student of immigration would benefit most from a visit to the national archives in Ottawa.

Finally, the reader is reminded that this directory includes only unpublished materials in archives and manuscript repositories. Even some of the most distinguished libraires in the United States and Canada do not have such collections for immigration of the groups we are focusing on. However, outstanding collections can be found in the U.S. National Archives in Washington, the Canadian Archives in Ottawa, New York Public Library, and the university libraries of Cornell, Michigan, Harvard, Duke, North Carolina, Samford University, and McGill.

HOW TO USE THIS DIRECTORY

This volume has entries for the United States first, followed by entries for Canada. The entries are numbered within the major national divisions, and entries appear alphabetically under the appropriate state or province, are arranged alphabetically by city, and are further alphabetized by name of the repository. The general index, which refers to entry numbers, provides reference to names of collections and to ethnic groups. To save space, we have made use of standard abbreviations within entries. A list of these follows.

ABBREVIATIONS

AL	Alabama
Alb	Alberta
AK	Alaska
AR	Arkansas
AZ	Arizona
BC	British Columbia
CA	California
CO	Colorado
CT	Connecticut
DAR	Daughters of the American Revolution
DC	District of Columbia
DCRMR	Directory of Canadian Records & Manuscripts Repositories
DE	Delaware
FARC	Federal Archives & Records Center
FL	Florida
GA	Georgia
Hamer	Philip Hamer's GUIDE TO ARCHIVES & MS COLLECTIONS IN THE U.S.
HI	Hawaii
HRS	Historical Records Survey
IA	Iowa
ID	Idaho
IL	Illinois
IN	Indiana
KS	Kansas
KY	Kentucky
LA	Louisiana
MA	Massachusetts
Man	Manitoba
MD	Maryland
ME	Maine
MI	Michigan
MN	Minnesota

MO	Missouri
ms	manuscript
MS	Mississippi
MT	Montana
NARC	National Archives & Records Service
NB	New Brunswick
NC	North Carolina
ND	North Dakota
NE	Nebraska
NH	New Hampshire
NHPRC	Directory of Archives & Manuscripts Repositories (US)
NJ	New Jersey
NM	New Mexico
NS	Nova Scotia
NSDAR	National Society of the Daughters of the American Revolution
NUCMC	National Union Catalogue of Manuscript Collections
NV	Nevada
NY	New York
OH	Ohio
OK	Oklahoma
Ont	Ontario
OR	Oregon
PA	Pennsylvania
PEI	Prince Edward Island
PR	Puerto Rico
QU	Quebec
RI	Rhode Island
Sas	Saskatchewan
SC	South Carolina
SD	South Dakota
TN	Tennessee

TX	Texas	WA	Washington
UT	Utah	WI	Wisconsin
VA	Virginia	WV	West Virginia
VI	Virgin Islands	WY	Wyoming
VT	Vermont	YT	Yukon Territory
w/	with		

United States Libraries
and Repositories

ALABAMA

1   BIRMINGHAM PUBLIC LIBRARY
          Department of Archives & Manuscripts
          2020 Park Place
          Birmingham, AL.   35203
          (205) 254-2698
     Hours: 9-6 M-Sat.
     Access: Open.
     Copying facilities.
Sources:
State of Alabama, Tenth Judicial Circuit Court, Immigration
& Naturalization Records, 1887-1911; Edith Ward Landon
Diaries, 1881-1933; Hill Ferguson Historical Collection
(family history volumes).

2   SAMFORD UNIVERSITY LIBRARY
          Special Collections Department
          Birmingham, AL.   35229
          (205) 870-2749
     Hours: 8-9 M.
            8-4:30 T-F.
     Access: In-house research by adults; queries must
            include a $20.00 advance deposit.
     Copying facilities.
Sources:
Albert E. Casey Collection of Irish materials (Cork and
Kerry & some other sections) - no name index but thousands
of names, births, deaths, & marriage records from Ireland;
Alabama manuscripts - 80 linear feet, 3,000 ms collections;
Baptist Convention records (1,200 records & diaries, plus
microfilm); Alabama newspapers on microfilm. Manuscript
collection is being microfilmed and will be available from
the Library Microfilm Dept.
Published finding aids: Albert E. Casey's O'Kief, Coshe-

Mang (Banner Press, Inc., 1980).

3.   HUNTSVILLE - MADISON COUNTY PUBLIC LIBRARY
           P.O. Box 443
           Huntsville, AL.   35804
           (205) 536-0021
       Hours: 9-9 M-Th.
              9-5 F-Sat.
              1-5 Sun.
       Access: Anyone under 14 must be accompanied by an
              adult.
       Copying facilities.
Sources:
Huntsville & Alabama heritage; Church & Bible records,
business records, correspondence, diaries and memoirs of
early Madison County settlers; Papers of Clement C. Clay
family; Papers of Maria Howard Weeden; several thousand
photographic prints.
Published finding aids: Southern Genealogy and History in
the Heritage Room: A Bibliography (1983).

4.   MOBILE PUBLIC LIBRARY
           Special Collections Division
           704 Government Street
           Mobile, AL.   36602
           (205) 438-7093
       Hours: 9-6 M-Sat.
       Access: Reference only. No interlibrary loan. Non-
              Mobile residents pay a $5.00 fee for 6-day
              pass.
       Copying facilities.
Sources:
Sizeable genealogical collection for South, North-East, and
East Coast (15,000 books, 4,500 census rolls); 1,200 family
histories; cemetary lists and death notices; numerous area
maps.
Published finding aids: None, but most items listed in card
catalogue; open stacks.

5.   ALABAMA DEPARTMENT OF ARCHIVES & HISTORY
           624 Washington Avenue
           Montgomery, AL.   36104
           (205) 261-4361
       Hours: 8-5 M-F.
              9-5 Sat.
       Access: No general restrictions.
       Copying facilities.
Sources:
Kate Cumming Collection (letters from family/friends in
Scotland); Lucretia Bailey Davidson Letters, 1860-82; John
Boyde Letter (from Belfast) to George Rives, 1843; James
Beer's British Consulate Pass, 1862; Raphael Semmes Collec-
tion, ca. 1860-90; Emory Bradley Indenture, 1813; Correspon-
dence of Cotton Dealers in Liverpool with Josiah Sibley &
Son, 1856-57, and 1866-67; William Ledford notebooks, offi-

cial records, from 1700, of the territory and state; county
records for all wars.
(See also NHPRC, Hamer, & NUCMC, 1959-61).
Published finding aids: None.

ALASKA

6.   UNIVERSITY OF ALASKA
            Anchorage Library
            Archives & Manuscript Department
            Anchorage, AK.   99504
            (907) 786-1849
        Hours: 8-5 M-F.
        Access: No general restrictions, but some collections
            are restricted.
        Copying facilities.
Sources:
Richard Tighe Harris Family Papers (include records from
County Down, and Ohio, Pennsylvania, Kansas, Idaho, Montana,
British Columbia, Missouri, & Alaska), 750 items from 1853-
1969; naturalization papers, correspondence, business records,
memoranda, genealogical notes, pictorial material & memorabi-
lia.
Published finding aids: Guide To The Family Papers Of Richard
Tighe Harris, Co-founder Of Juneau Alaska (Anchorage Library,
1981).

7.   ALASKA STATE ARCHIVES & LIBRARY
            141 Willoughby Avenue
            Juneau, AK.   99801
Sources:
No relevant ms sources, but see FARC in Seattle for Alaska
materials.

ARIZONA

8.   MESA ARIZONA BRANCH GENEALOGICAL LIBRARY
            464 East 1st Avenue
            Mesa, AZ.   85204
            (602) 964-1200
        Hours: 9-5 M, F, & Sat.
               9-9 T, W, & Th.
        Access: Open.
        Copying facilities.
Sources:
(Branch of Genealogical Library, Salt Lake City). Several
thousand rolls of microfilm & microfiche, 220 volumes of
family records (pedigree charts and family group records),

1,500 published biographies and family histories, and 1,000
published volumes of Parish Records.
Published finding aids: None, but all materials are cross-
referenced in the card catalogue.

9.   ARIZONA DEPARTMENT OF LIBRARY, ARCHIVES & PUBLIC
      RECORDS
            3rd Floor Capitol
            1700 West Washington
            Phoenix, AZ.   85007
            (602) 255-3942
      Hours: 8-5 M-F.
      Access: Open shelves; non-circulation, but will photo-
            copy if surnames/subjects given.
Sources:
Printed volumes only of Irish and Irish-American related
materials.
Published finding aids: None.

10.   ARIZONA STATE UNIVERSITY
            Tempe, AZ. 85287
Sources:
Questionnaire not returned.

11.   ARIZONA HERITAGE CENTER
            Division of Arizona Historical Society
            949 East Second Street
            Tucson, AZ.   85719
            (602) 628-5774
      Hours: 10-4 M-F.
             10-1 Sat.
      Access: Non-circulating.
Sources:
Pioneers in Arizona Collection, Great Registers (See also
University of Arizona, Arizona State University, & local
historical societies); Lori Davisson Notebooks and Indexes
of Scottish Materials (clippings, copies of diaries, photographs, census data, & places of birth) includes family
names from Alexander to Williams.
Published finding aids: None.

12.   UNIVERSITY OF ARIZONA
            Tucson, AZ. 85721
Sources:
Questionnaire not returned.

ARKANSAS

13.   ARKANSAS HISTORY COMMISSION
            One Capitol Mall
            Little Rock, AR.   72201
            (501) 371-2141

Hours: 10-4 M-F.
Access: By permission.
Copying facilities.
Sources:
Indexes to passenger arrival records for Atlantic (excluding
New York) and Gulf Coast ports 1820-74, and for New Orleans,
1853-99, on 220 rolls of microfilm (data includes name, age,
marital status, nationality, date of arrival, destination,
and name of the vessel); census records, military records,
& newspaper files; 75 Arkansas county records, 1797-1920
(marriages, estates, deeds, & court); newspaper files, 1819
- present.
Published finding aids: None.

CALIFORNIA

14.   CALIFORNIA STATE UNIVERSITY, FRESNO
            Department of Special Collections
            Henry Madden Library
            Fresno, CA.   93740
            (209) 294-2595
       Hours: 10-5 M-F.
       Access: No restrictions.
       Copying facilities.
Sources:
Fresno city records (block books 1888-1900; ordinances, 1904
-1966; & resolutions, 1923-1966), and county records (including assessment rolls, 1856-1889; tax books, 1885-1897; real
estate checks and plat books, 1884-1901; and certificates
of sales for taxes, 1875-1888).
Published finding aids: None.

15.   FRESNO COUNTY FREE LIBRARY
            2420 Mariposa
            Fresno, CA.   93721
            (209) 488-3195
       Hours: 9-9 M & T.
              9-6 W & F.
              12-9 Th.
              1-5 Sat.
       Access: Open.
       Copying facilities.
Sources:
Fresno Genealogical Society Collection; voter registration
records, city ordinances, oral history - 250 interview
transcriptions, standard genealogical research tools.
Published finding aids: None.

16.   FEDERAL ARCHIVES & RECORD CENTER
            c/o Regional Archivist
            24000 Avila Road
            Laguna Niguel, CA.   92677

(714) 831-4220
Hours: 8-4:30 M-F.
Access: Most collections open.
Copying facilities.
Sources:
(Serves AZ, counties of southern CA, and Clark Co. NV.)
Records of District Courts of U.S. (Civil, Criminal, Admiral-
ty, & Bankruptcy) until the 1950's; Records of United Courts
of Appeals, 1891-1950's; Records of Bureau of Customs; Re-
cords of Office of the Chief of Engineers; census records;
NARC Microfilms (genealogy/ethnology).
Published finding aids: Research Opportunities (General
Services Administration: National Archives and Records
Service, 1980).

17.   PASADENA PUBLIC LIBRARY
            Genealogy Room
            285 E. Walnut Street
            Pasadena, CA.   91101
            (818) 405-4052
        Hours: 9-9   M-Th.
               9-6   F & Sat.
               1-5   Sun.
        Access: Open.
        Copying facilities.
Sources:
California census of 1852; shelf-list of California State
Library, Sacramento Sutro Branch; Cox, Darnell, Dennison,
Holder, Jewett, Monroe, and other families; published family
histories; genealogical & historical periodicals.
Published finding aids: Joyce Y. Pinney's Genealogical Quest:
A Pasadena Bibliography (PPL, 1977).

18.   CALIFORNIA STATE ARCHIVES
            1020 O Street
            Sacramento, CA.   95814
            (916) 445-4293
        Hours: 8-5 M-F.
        Access: Most collections open.
        Copying facilities.
Sources:
1852 California State Census, and 1860 & 1880 U.S. Censuses
for California, special censuses of California cities and
towns for 1897-1938; military records, 1849-1945; executive
records, secretary of state records, controller's records,
legislative records, and court records, 1850-present; Department of Education records, 1863-1920; vital statistics (birth,
marriage, death) July 1, 1905-present.
Published finding aids: Genealogical Research In The California State Archives (Sacramento, n.d.).

19.   FEDERAL ARCHIVES & RECORDS CENTER
            c/o Regional Archivist
            1000 Commodore Drive
            San Bruno, CA.   94066
            (415) 876-9009

Hours: 8-4:30   M, T, Th, & F.
        8-8   W.
Access: Most collections open.
Copying facilities.
Sources:
(Serves CA, except southern CA, HI, NV, except Clark Co, &
Pacific Ocean area). Records of District Courts of U.S.
(Civil, Criminal, Admiralty, and Bankruptcy) until the
1950's; Records of United Courts of Appeals, 1891-1950's;
Records of Bureau of Indian Affairs; Records of Bureau of
Customs; Records of Office of Chief of Engineers; Records
of Government of American Samoa, 1899-1965; census records;
NARC Microfilms (genealogy/ethnology).
Published finding aids: Research Opportunities (General
Services Administration: National Archives and Records
Service, 1980).

20.   SAN DIEGO PUBLIC LIBRARY
          Genealogy Room & California Room
          820 E Street
          San Diego, CA.   92101-6478
          (619) 236-5834
      Hours: 10-9 Th.
             9:30-5:30 F & Sat.
      Access: Reference only.
      Copying facilities.
Sources:
Great Register of Voters of San Diego County, 1866-1908
(California Room; lists country of origin); family data on
Adamson, Baker, Dixon, Drake, Kimball, Knill, Williams, and
others. (See also: Mormon Genealogical Library and San Diego
Genealogical Society Library).
Published finding aids: None.

21.   SANTA BARBARA MISSION ARCHIVE LIBRARY
          Old Mission
          Santa Barbara, CA.   93105
          (805) 682-4713
      Hours: 9-5 T-Sat.
      Access: Open.
      Copying facilities.
Sources:
Mostly Hispanic California records, 1769-1848, but see De La
Guerra Family Papers (Hartnell Connection) and pioneer regis-
ter in final section of volumes 2 & 5 of Hubert Howe Bancroft
History of California, 1884-1890; baptismal, marriage, and
death registers of most of the twenty-one California missions.
Published finding aids: None, but calendars of documents and
indexes to each collection.

22.   SUTRA LIBRARY, BRANCH OF CALIFORNIA STATE LIBRARY
          480 Winston Drive
          San Francisco, CA.   94132
          (415) 731-4477
      Hours: 10-5 M-F.
      Access: Open.

Copying facilities.
Sources:
Family history & local history collections for all states
except California (for California, see entries 14-20); ship
passenger sources; British local history and genealogy;
Genealogical Card Catalogue (48 negative microfiche).
Published finding aids: Local History & Genealogy Resources
of the California State Library and Its Sutra Branch (n.d.).
Users Guide To The Sutra Library Family History & Local
History Subject Catalogues (n.d.).

23.   STANFORD UNIVERSITY LIBRARY
          Hoover Institute of War, Revolution & Peace
          Stanford, CA. 94305
          (415) 497-3563
          Hours: 8-5 M-F.
                 9-1 Sat.
          Access: Open for in-house use; some interlibrary loan.
          Copying facilities.
Sources:
James A. Healy Collection (letters by Sean T. Kelly, Alice
Stopford Green, Bulmer Hobson, and Joseph McGarrity); special
newspaper issues from 1896-1966; Roger Casement materials;
A.J. and Ann Monday Collection (pamphlets, leaflets, posters,
& photographs relating to Ulster conflict, 1969-present).
Published finding aids: Agnes F. Peterson, Survey of the
Hoover Institute Collection (Stanford, 1976).

COLORADO

24.   COLORADO COLLEGE
          Library, Special Collections
          Colorado Springs, CO. 80903
          (303) 473-2233
          Hours: 9-4 M-F.
          Access: Open, with permission.
          Copying facilities.
Sources:
(NUCMC 1967, '76, & Hamer, 1961, p. 47).
400 items ("200 ms & letters of English poets, 50 autographs
and ltrs of prominent 19th c. Americans, & 50 ltrs & documents pertaining to American Revolution, French Revolution,
U.S. Civil War, and American Founding Fathers" - Hamer, 1961,
p. 47).
Published finding aids: None.

25.   COLORADO DIVISION OF STATE ARCHIVES & PUBLIC RECORDS
          1313 Sherman Street, Rm. 1-B-20
          Denver, CO.   80203
          (303) 866-2055
          Hours: 8-4:45 M-F.
          Access: Varies with the record. Patron must have

written permission from depositing agency to
use closed materials.
Copying facilities.
Sources:
Public records of the State of Colorado; statewide marriage
index, 1900-1939, some counties and cities, 1861-1975; court
records (divorce and probate); naturalization records, 1862
-1941; military records, 1861-1949; census records - Colorado
State, 1885, U.S. - 1860, 1870, 1880, & 1900; birth (1910-
on) and death (1900-on) records.
Published finding aids: Guide To The Resources Of The Colorado State Archives (n.d.).

26.   COLORADO STATE HISTORICAL SOCIETY LIBRARY
          1300 Broadway
          Denver, CO.   80203
          (303) 866-3682
       Hours: 9-5 M-F.
       Access: Open to adults.
       Copying facilities.
Sources:
Lizzie Mahan Gaynor (150 items - correspondence, 1878-1907,
11 diaries, 1886-1921; school recitations, diplomas, maps,
& photographs); Henry Colbran (48 items - correspondence,
1958-69, personal & business documents, manuscripts, clippings
& photographs); Prairie Cattle Co., Ltd. (493 items, including
correspondence, 1900-1917, and business papers, 1880-1917);
Patrick Boyle (70 items - clippings, passport, 1932, & others);
Lydia Franklin Sudbury Goodaker (5 items); William Shires
(diary, 1862).
Published finding aids: None.

27.   FEDERAL ARCHIVES & RECORDS CENTER
          c/o Regional Archivist
          Building 48, Denver Federal Center
          Denver CO.   80255
          (303) 236-0818
       Hours: 7:30-4:30 M-F.
       Access: Most collections open.
       Copying facilities.
Sources:
(Serves CO, MT, ND, SD, UT, & WY). Records of District Courts
of U.S. (Civil, Criminal, Admiralty, & Bankruptcy) until the
1950's; Records of United Courts of Appeals, 1891-1950's;
Records of Bureau of Indian Affairs; Records of Bureau of
Customs; Records of Office of the Chief of Engineers; Census
Records, NARC Microfilms (genealogy/ethnology).
Published finding aids: Research Opportunities (General
Services Administration: National Archives & Records Service,
1980).

28.   DENVER PUBLIC LIBRARY
          Western History Collection
          1357 Broadway
          Denver, CO. 80203
          (303) 571-2009

Hours: 10-9 M,T,W.
          10-5:30 F & Sat.
Access: Must apply and be approved; $20.00 fee for
          non-Denver residents.
Copying facilities, but with some restrictions on
          copying.
Sources:
"English Sporting Man's Diary" (381 pp., 1884-85); James
Duncan letter 1910 (Clan Gordon Pipe Band); Journal of Mrs.
Wm. Abraham Bell (nee Cara), 1872-76; newspapers & micro-
film. (See NUCMC & Hamer).
Published finding aids: Western History Brochure (DPL, n.d.).

CONNECTICUT

29.   BRIDGEPORT PUBLIC LIBRARY
          Historical Collections
          925 Broad Street
          Bridgeport, CT.   06604
          (203) 576-7417
       Hours: 9-5 M-Sat.
          Closed in summer.
       Access: Open.
       Copying facilities.
Sources:
Collections of family papers for Bridgeport and surrounding
towns including: Roger M. Sherman, 1793-1844; Henry A. House,
1860-1927; Reverend Samuel Orcutt & Benjamin L. Swan, 1841-
1893; and Ethan Ferris Bishop, 1851-1897; business papers
include Locomobile Company of America, 1900-1928; John &
Julius Benham, 1845-1862, Patrick O'Rourke, 1879-1893, &
Henry Sanford, 1894-1901; military records, 1784-1945; organization records, 1877-1976; city archives, 1793-1976; newspapers, 1795-date; P.T. Barnum Collection, 1832-1888.
Published finding aids: "Notes on the Historical Collections
of the Bridgeport Public Library" (Connecticut History, Oct.,
1977, No. 20; rptd. Bridgeport Public Library, Dec., 1977).

30.   CONNECTICUT HISTORICAL SOCIETY LIBRARY
          1 Elizabeth Street
          Hartford, CT.   06105
          (203) 236-5621
       Hours: 9-5 M-F.
          9-5 Sat. (during summer)
       Access: Identification - drivers license or other I.D.
          required.
       Copying facilities, but ms may be photocopied by staff
          members only.
Sources:
Booth Brothers Quarriers, 1871-91 (2 boxes of orders, bills,
correspondence); 17 March 1858 address by William Downes -
"Irish Adopted Citizens, Their Position - Civil and Religious".

Other letters, diaries, manuscripts, photos, & microfilm
on Connecticut people; copies of church, town, and public
records grouped by town; business and club records. Access
to the collection by family name.
Published finding aids: None.

31.   CONNECTICUT STATE LIBRARY
           Archives, History & Genealogy Unit
           231 Capital Avenue
           Hartford, CT.   06106
           (203) 566-3690
       Hours: 8:30-5 M-F.
              9-1   Sat.
       Access: Open, but only bound volumes are available on
               Saturday.
       Copying facilities.
Sources:
Naturalization records (Boxes 585-602) and records of the
Works Projects Administration, Conn., 1935-44 - Ethnic Groups
Survey (edited copy of papers on ethnic groups, 1936-38,
Files on study of organizations, 1936-40, interviews, scrap-
books, and working papers on British/English, Irish, and
other ethnic groups.
Published finding aids: Record of the Works Project Adminis-
tration, Connecticut, 1935-44 (CSL, 22 Sept., 1972) and
Court Records in the Connecticut State Library, 1636-1945
(CSL, June 1981).

32.   GODFREY MEMORIAL LIBRARY
           134 Newfield Street
           Middletown, CT.   06457
           (203) 346-4375
       Hours: 9-4 M-F.
       Access: On-premise use only.
       Copying facilities.
Sources:
Family records and data on Bacon, Bell, Brooks, Camp, Church,
Cole, Converse, Hawley, Heath, Hodge, Holliday, Rider, Rob-
inson, Scott-Keating, Seymour, Sherman, & Thompson (Identi-
fies England or Ireland as country of origin).
Published finding aids: None.

33.   NEW HAVEN COLONY HISTORICAL SOCIETY
           Whitney Library
           114 Whitney Avenue
           New Haven, CT.   06417
           (203) 562-4183
       Hours: 10-4:45 T-F.
       Access: Open.
       Copying facilities.
Sources:
Jared Ingersall Papers; Ezra Stiles Papers; payrolls, muster
rolls, & other Revolutionary War materials; logbooks and
journals from the 1839 Wilkes Expedition to the Anarctic;
logbooks and diaries for sea voyages, 1795-1850.
Published finding aids: None.

34.   YALE UNIVERSITY LIBRARY
           Manuscripts & Archives
           Box 1603 A Yale Station/121 Wall Street
           New Haven, CT. 06520
           (203) 432-4694
       Hours: 8:30-4:45 M-F.
       Access: Two pieces of I.D. required for registration.
       Copying facilities.
Sources:
(See NUCMC & Research Libraries Information Network On-Line
Computer Catalog). No special collections on immigration
from England, Scotland, Ireland, and Wales, but materials on
specific families and organizations; American Colonial Col-
lections; documentation of the Yale family of Chester and
Wales, and the Pierpont family. See Historical ms collections
(Hamer, pp. 61-67), and Western Americana Collection (Hamer,
pp. 69-70).
Published finding aids: See Above.

35.   FERGUSON LIBRARY
           96 Broad Street
           Stamford, CT. 06901
           (203) 964-1000
       Hours: 9-9 M-F.
              9-5:30 Sat.
              1-5 Sun. (Oct. - May)
       Access: Open.
       Copying facilities.
Sources:
City directories, 1872-present; local newspapers, 1829-pre-
sent; large local photograph collection; "Stamford File" of
clippings and uncatalogued local history material & large
genealogy manuscript collection; Barbour Collection (119
rolls of microfilm of early vital records for Conn., census
microfilm for Conn.). Collection oriented to Connecticut;
Westchester/ Putnam/ Dutchess counties in New York.
Published finding aids: Thomas J. Kemp, Genealogies in the
Ferguson Library (Stamford, 1982).

DELAWARE

36.   DELAWARE STATE ARCHIVES
           Hall of Records
           Dover, DE. 19901
           (302) 736-5318
       Hours: 8:30-4:15 T-F.
              8-12:30 & 1-3:45 Sat.
       Access: Open.
       Copying facilities.
Sources:
Non-current records, 1655-present (most from 19th century)
State (executive 1776-present, legislative 1776-present,

judicial, 1700-on); County (land warrants, surveys, deeds, 1640-1870; probate records, 1676-1916; vital statistics, 1713-1913); Municipal (Wilmington, Dover, Georgetown, Viola, Magnolia, and Frederica); Manuscript collections - Ridgely Papers, John Dickinson Collection, and private accounts collection (business records of storekeepers, farmers, craftsmen, and professional men - 18th century-on); correspondence of George Read, Caesar Rodney, John M. Clayton, et. al.; also manuscript genealogies.
Published finding aids: DOC # 20-06/83/08/10.

37.   ELEUTHERIAN MILLS HISTORICAL SOCIETY
          P.O. Box 3630, Greenville
          Wilmington, DE.   19807
          (302) 658-2401 / (215) 627-3991
       Hours: 8:30-4:30 M-F.
       Access: Write before visiting.
       Copying facilities.
Sources:
E.I. duPont deNemours & Co. Records (letter books, 1805-1857, 42 volumes); P.S. duPont Office Collection (article on Irish powderworkers, 1839); Farnum Collection; Joseph Shipley Papers (records of passage, Londonderry to Wilmington, 1827); Longwood Manuscripts (correspondence concerning Irish labor, 1803; production of gunpowder in Ireland; 1802-15 ledgers, bills, and accounts of workers; employee records, 1803-1917); Joseph Robinson Inventory; Eleuthera Bradford Collection, 1803-32 (rules for workers, wage sheets, medical bills); Winterthur ms (correspondence 1803-1866); Reverend Patrick Kenny (diary, personal & parochial records, 1805-1828); Christ Church School Merit Board, 1817; Hagley Museum Oral Interview Program, 1955-1974; National Archives Census Returns, 1820, 1830.
Published finding aids: Guide to Manuscripts (EMHL, n.d.).

38.   HISTORICAL SOCIETY OF DELAWARE
          505 Market Street
          Wilmington, DE.   19801
          (302) 655-7161
       Hours: 1-9 M.
              9-5 T-F.
       Access: Open.
       Copying facilities.
Sources:
New Castle County Naturalization Records, 1826-1858; Bancroft Family Papers (19th cent. English Quaker); Passengers arriving at Wilmington, 1828-1849; lists of passengers in Wilmington newspapers, 1780's-on; records of Welsh Tract Baptist Meeting; Descendents of Early Welsh Tract Families.
Published finding aids: None.

DISTRICT OF COLUMBIA

39.   CATHOLIC UNIVERSITY OF AMERICA
            Dept. of Archives and Manuscripts
            6th & Michigan Ave., N.E.
            Washington, D.C.   20064
            (202) 635-5-65
        Hours: 9-5 M-F
        Access: Subject to archivist's approval.
        Copying facilities.
Sources:
1885 - date (4,000 linear feet and 75 rolls of microfilm);
(See Hamer, pp. 81-82, and NHPRC Directory of Archives &
Manuscript Repositories, p. 113). Papers of faculty and
other Catholics; labor records; records of Fenian Brotherhood, 1859-1904.
Published finding aids: Henry J. Browne, "Manuscript Collections at the Catholic University of America," in Manuscripts, 6: 166-168 (Spring, 1954).

40.   DAR (NATIONAL SOCIETY OF DAUGHTERS OF THE AMERICAN
      REVOLUTION) LIBRARY
            1776 D Street, N.W.
            Washington, D.C. 20006-5392
            (202) 628-1776
        Hours: 9-4 M-F.
        Access: Daily entrance fee for non-members; otherwise,
                open.
        Copying facilities.
Sources:
Genealogical Records Committee Reports (several thousand
volumes of typescript prepared by DAR members, all states;
documentary proofs of lineage claims), with focus on American families.
Published finding aids: DAR Library Catalog, Volume One:
Family Histories and Genealogies (1982, 1983), DAR Library
Catalog, Supplement To Volume One (1984); two others on
state and local histories and records projected (perhaps
1985).

41.   GEORGETOWN UNIVERSITY
            John Reynolds Library
            Washington, D.C.   20057
            (202) 625-4095
        Hours: 9-5 M-F.
        Access: Open.
Sources:
Americana Collection includes Archives of Md. Province
Jesuits, 1640-1870, records of individual Jesuits; Parish
records (Baptisms - not indexed); Robert Wagner Papers;
Eugene McCarthy Papers.
Published finding aids: None.

42.   LIBRARY OF CONGRESS
            Manuscript Division
            Washington, D.C.   20540
            (202) 287-5387
        Hours: 8:30-5 M-Sat.
        Access: Open to graduate students & others, various
            types of restrictions on access.
        Copying facilities.
Sources:
Amory Family Papers (1,400 items, 1697-1823); James O.
Halliwell-Phillipps Collection (7,000 British documents,
1632-1750); Theophilus Harris Papers (70 items, 1793-1934);
National Library of Ireland Papers (microfilm of 1,400 items
relating to America); Sir Thomas Phillipps Collection (4,200
items relating to British in North America); William Sampson
Papers (Ireland & America, 1806-49); Sterritt Family Papers
(1798-1859), a Scottish family in Kentucky & Virginia;
Littleton Dennis Teachle's Diary (6 vols., 1799-1800, travels
in Britain); William Wakefield Collection (17,200 English
legal documents, 1399-1908); Richard A. Wynill's Memoir
(British Army, 1778-c. 1814).
Other finding aids:
Annual Report Of The Librarian Of Congress, 1897-date
L.C. Quarterly Journal Of Current Acquisitions, 1943-date
National Union Catalogue Of MS Collections, 1959-date

43.   LIBRARY OF CONGRESS
            Rare Book & Special Collections Division
            110 1st Street, S.E.
            Washington, D.C.   20540
            (202) 287-5434
        Hours: 8:30-5 M-F.
        Access: At least 18 years of age; one current I.D.
        Copying facilities.
Sources:
Charles A. Banks Collection (37 volumes - 17th century Eng-
lish migration to America) includes "Notes from Genealogical
Gleanings in England" (a series of completed family histories),
"Topographical Dictionary of the English Settlers in America"
(places of origin), tax rolls (geographical by counties -
name of tax payer and his address), and miscellaneous volumes
of London marriage records and individual family histories.
Published finding aids: None.

44.   NATIONAL ARCHIVES AND RECORDS SERVICES
            Office of National Archives
            8th Street & Pennsylvania Ave., N.W.
            Washington, D.C.   20408
            (202) 523-3218
        Hours: 8:45-5:15 M-F.
        Access: Restrictions described in General Information
            Leaflets # 2 & 27.
        Copying facilities.
Sources:
800,000 cu. ft. of records (largely Federal) from the American Revolutionary period to the present time (see Hamer's

Guide To Archives & MS In U.S., 1961, pp. 125-128, for full
annotation).
Published finding aids: Numerous. See Guide To The Records
In The National Archives (1948, 648 p.), supplemented by
National Archives Accessions.

45.   NATIONAL GENEALOGICAL SOCIETY LIBRARY
            1921 Sunderland Place, N.W.
            Washington, D.C.   20036
            (202) 785-2123
      Hours: 11-4 M-W-F.
             & 7-9 W
      Access: Free for members; $2.00 fee, non-members.
      Copying facilities.
Sources:
Includes ms materials donated by society members (family &
local historians, cemetery records, Bible records, etc.)
some 15,000 volumes.
Published finding aids: NGS Booklist, 1978; Supplement to
Booklist, 1983.

46.   NATIONAL GEOGRAPHIC SOCIETY LIBRARY
            16 & M Streets, N.W.
            Washington, D.C.   20036
            (202) 857-7787/ 857-7784
      Hours: 8:30-5 M-F.
      Access: Reading Room - open to the public; stacks -
             only by special permission.
      Copying facilities.
Sources:
Geographical/cultural collection (guidebooks, geographies,
encyclopedias, biographies, and general books on various
areas), and a clipping service (vertical file) on all
aspects of countries.
Published finding aids: None.

FLORIDA

47.   GAINESVILLE PUBLIC LIBRARY
            222 East University Ave.
            Gainesville, FL.   32601
            (904) 374-2091
      Hours: 10-9 M-Th.
             10-5 F-Sat.
             1-5 Sun.
      Copying facilities.
Sources:
Alachua County Cemetery Records (3 volumes, indexed by family
name); Jess Davis's History of Alachua County, 1963, and
History of Gainesville, Florida, 1965 (typescripts of over-
lapping vols.); Charles Halsey Hildreth's History of Gainesville, Florida, 1954 (doctoral dissertation); Index and

Obituary Index to the <u>Gainesville Sun</u> (newspaper).
Published finding aids: None.

48.   UNIVERSITY OF FLORIDA
          P.K. Younge Library of Florida History
          404 Library West
          Gainesville, FL.   32611
          (904) 392-0319
       Hours: 8-4:45 M-F.
       Access: Adult examination only; not all materials can
              be copied.
       Copying facilities.
Sources:
Large collection of microfilm of colonial Florida materials
from London Public Record Office (Colonial Office & Audit
Office Papers, 1763-84, for Provinces of East & West Florida);
microfilm of Florida-related materials in Thomas Gage Papers,
Sir Guy Carleton Papers, Sir Frederick Handiman Collection,
and the Fulham Papers; microfilm of East Florida Papers
(government records of Spanish province of East Florida,
1784-1821); microfilm copies of papers relating to West
Florida from the Papeles de Cuba (archives, Seville, Spain);
Calendars To The East Florida Papers and The West Florida
Materials.
Published finding aids: Calendars noted above.

49.   ORANGE COUNTY LIBRARY SYSTEM
          Genealogy Department
          10 North Rosalind Avenue
          Orlando, FL.   32801
          (303) 425-4694
       Hours: 9-9 M-F.
              9-6 Sat.
              1-5 Sun.
       Access: Open; materials non-circulating.
       Copying facilities.
Sources:
B. Brown Commander Collection (2 file cabinets, 25 or 30
families, including Commander, Stephens & Vineyard); 600
family histories; cemetery records; family newsletters.
Published finding aids: None.

50.   UNIVERSITY OF WEST FLORIDA
          John C. Pace Library
          Pensacola, FL.   32504
          (904) 474-2424
       Hours: 8-5 M-F.
       Access: Open.
       Copying facilities.
Sources:
J.J. Sullivan & Son Collection (legal papers, correspondence,
& deeds, 1885-1929, for Escambia & Santa Rosa Counties) and
Jones Family Papers (legal, political, & family papers for
Irish-born U.S. Senator Charles W. Jones, 1834-1897).
Published finding aids: None.

51.   UNIVERSITY OF SOUTH FLORIDA LIBRARY
          Special Collections
          Tampa, FL. 33620
          (813) 974-2731
       Hours: 8-5 M-F.
       Access: Open.
       Copying facilities.
Sources:
Shipton Family Letters (11 letters written to Thomas Ship-
ton from his mother, brother, and sister in England, 1794-
1816).
Published finding aids: None.

GEORGIA

52.   ATLANTA HISTORICAL SOCIETY
          3101 Andrews Drive, N.W.
          Atlanta, GA. 30305
          (404) 621-1837
       Hours: 9-5 M-F.
       Access: Open.
       Copying facilities.
Sources:
Focus on Atlanta & surrounding area; vertical file series
of genealogical materials more useful to those pursuing
family histories than to students of immigration or of mass
population shifts.
Published finding aids: Louise D. Cook's Guide To The Manuscript Collection Of The Atlanta Historical Society (Atlanta,
1976).

53.   GEORGIA DEPARTMENT OF ARCHIVES AND HISTORY
          330 Capitol Avenue, S.E.
          Atlanta, GA. 30334
          (404) 656-2358
       Hours: 8-4:30 M-F.
              9:30-3:30 Sat.
       Access: Must receive visitor's pass.
       Copying facilities.
Sources:
4,000 cubic feet of original probate, marriage, & other
county records; 19,000 reels of microfilm of vital, land,
probate, and other county records (1732-present); land grant
surveys, maps & plats; Attorney General's records relating
to Revolutionary War & other; papers of various organizations
and individuals.
Published finding aids: Mary Givens Bryan, Report by the
Georgia Dept. of Archives & History on ... Activities in
Georgia (1955, 65 pp.).

54.   BRADLEY MEMORIAL LIBRARY
           Genealogical & Historical Room
           1120 Bradley Drive
           Columbus, GA. 31995
           (404) 327-0211
           Hours: 10-5 M-F.
           Access: Open.
           Copying facilities.
Sources:
Family file; Births & Deaths file; State file (most states);
family genealogies; family histories; State & County his-
tories; church records (local); funeral records (local);
Census Indexes (1790-1850) and microfilms (AL., GA., N.C.,
S.C., PA., VA., KY., & MS.).
Published finding aids: None.

55.   FEDERAL ARCHIVES AND RECORDS CENTER
           c/o Regional Archivist
           1557 St. Joseph Avenue
           East Point, GA. 30344
           (404) 763-7477
           Hours: 8-5 M-F.
           Access: Most collections open.
           Copying facilities.
Sources:
(Serves AL., GA., FL., KY., MS., N.C., TN., & S.C.); Re-
cords of District Courts of U.S. (Civil, Criminal, Admiralty,
& Bankruptcy) until the 1950's; Records of United Courts of
Appeals, 1891-1950's; Records of Bureau of Indian Affairs;
Records of Bureau of Customs; Records of Office of the Chief
of Engineers; census records; NARC Microfilms (genealogy/
ethnology); 24,000,000 registration cards for the U.S. Draft,
1917-18.
Published finding aids: Research Opportunities (General
Services Administration: National Archives and Records
Service, 1980).

HAWAII

56.   ALOHA MEMORIAL LIBRARY (NSDAR)
           1914 Makiki Heights Drive
           Honolulu, HI. 96822
           (808) 946-6833
           Hours: 9-12 (Noon) Th.& Sat.
           Access: Open.
           Copying facilities.
Sources:
1790 census records (most states) & later; family histories;
ship passenger lists; Early London Grant Maps of S.C.; DAR
& SAR Records; periodicals and books; records of N.H., VT.,
MA., N.Y., PA., VA., S.C., N.C., GA., OH., KY., TN., LA., & AL.

Published finding aids: None.

57.   HAWAIIAN HISTORICAL SOCIETY
          560 Kawaiohao Street
          Honolulu, HI.   96813
          (808) 537-6271
          Hours: 10-4 M-F.
          Access: Open, but materials do not circulate.
          Copying facilities.
Sources:
(Focus on political, economic & social history of Hawaii
from 1778 to early 20th century). Materials include 19th
cent. newspapers published in Hawaii; photograph collection
(1880-1930); hand drawn maps of the islands, and harbor and
oil paintings; Journal of Hiram Bingham, Jr.; Diary of William Cooper Parke; 1817 account book of William French;
correspondence of Joel Turrill and Serena Bishop; travel
notes of Gorham Gilman; papers of W.D. Alexander; research
notes of N.B. Emerson and J.F. Stokes.
Published finding aids: Helen Lind (ed.) Voyages To Hawaii
Before 1860 (UHP, 1974); Hawaiian Language Imprints, 1822-
1899: A Bibliography (UHP, 1978); and Directory of Historical Records Repositories in Hawaii (Honolulu, H.H.S., 1982).

58.   HAWAII STATE ARCHIVES
          Iolani Palace Grounds
          Honolulu, HI.   96813
          (808) 548-2355
          Hours: 7:45-4:30 M-F.
          Access: Open.
          Copying facilities.
Sources:
Immigration records, 1842-1900; court records, 1842 - date;
marriage records, 1842-date, most since 1896; tax records;
naturalization records, 1844-94; city directories; and
business records.
Published finding aids: Searching Genealogical Records In
Hawaii (HSA, 1982).

IDAHO

59.   IDAHO STATE HISTORICAL SOCIETY
          Division of Manuscripts & Archives
          610 N. Julia Davis Drive
          Boise, ID.   83706
          (208) 334-3356
Sources:
No relevant materials; Scandinavian & Manuscript Collections
ONLY.

ILLINOIS

60.   CHICAGO HISTORICAL SOCIETY
           Clark Street at North Avenue
           Chicago, IL. 60614
           (312) 642-4600
       Hours: 9:30-4:30 T-Sat.
       Access: Fee for non-members.
       Copying facilities.
Sources:
George W. Snow Letters to 1870; Roger T. Faherty Papers,
1889-1967; John Frederick Finerty Papers, 1846-1908; John
Munn Journal, 1824-73; James A. Mulligan Collection, 1830-
64; Frank Conlan Collection, 1874 -; Harpel Scrapbook;
Benton House records; political records; business records;
historical period collections; Irish Club & Society records.
Published finding aids: None.

61.   FEDERAL ARCHIVES AND RECORDS CENTER
           c/o Regional Archivist
           7358 South Pulaski Road
           Chicago, IL. 60629
           (312) 581-7816
       Hours: 8-4:30 M-F.
       Access: Most collections open.
       Copying facilities.
Sources:
(Serves IL., IN., MI., MN., OH., & WI.). Records of District
Courts of U.S. (Civil, Criminal, Admiralty, & Bankruptcy)
until the 1950's; Records of United Courts of Appeals, 1891-
1950's; Records of Bureau of Indian Affairs; Records of
Bureau of Customs; Records of Office of the Chief of Engineers;
census records; NARC Microfilms (genealogy/ethnology).
Published finding aids: <u>Research Opportunities</u> (General Services Administration: National Archives & Records Service,
1980).

62.   ILLINOIS STATE ARCHIVES
           Archives Building
           Springfield, IL. 62756
           (217) 782-3556
       Hours: 8-4:30 M-F.
              8-3   Sat.
       Access: By registration.
       Copying facilities.
Sources:
Territorial and State records from 1812; transcripts and descriptions of many county archives; Federal Census records
for Illinois; naturalization records for some counties in
Regional Archives; copies of published local histories.
Published finding aids: <u>Descriptive Inventory of the Archives
of the State of Illinois</u> (ISA, n.d.); <u>A Guide to County Records in the Illinois Regional Archives</u> (ISA, n.d.).

63.   ILLINOIS STATE HISTORICAL LIBRARY
           Old State Capitol
           Springfield, IL.   62706
           (217) 782-4836
       Hours: 8:30-5 M-F.
       Access: Open.
       Copying facilities.
Sources:
David King Family Papers, 1798-1927; Flower Family Papers,
1816-1960's; Philander Chase Papers, 1775-1852, including
1,500 items; McConnell Letters, 1838-74; Federal Writers
Project Records, 1935-1944; others.
Published finding aids: None.

64.   ILLINOIS STATE HISTORICAL SOCIETY
           Old State Capitol
           Springfield, IL.   62706
           (217) 782-4836
       Hours: 8:30-5 M-F.
       Access: Open.
       Copying facilities.
Sources:
County plat books, 1870-1930; indexes and census reports;
vertical file on Illinois families; microfilms of newspaper
collections; journals; quarterlies; newsletters from many
organizations.
Published finding aids: None.

INDIANA

65.   ALLEN COUNTY PUBLIC LIBRARY
           Genealogy Department
           900 Webster Street/ P.O. Box 2270
           Fort Wayne, IN.   46801
           (219) 424-7241
       Hours: 9-9 M-Th.
              9-6 F-Sat.
       Access: Non-circulating.
       Copying facilities.
Sources:
Microfilm holdings include all available U.S. Census Schedules
from 1790-1910 for all states and Canadian Census for 1825-
1881; passenger lists (1820 -) for East Coast ports; N.C.
County records (Core Collection); local records for OH., TN.,
WV., & others; city directories from 1700's through 1901;
pension and bounty applications (Revolutionary War - on);
general histories of Scotland, parish and town records; parish
registers and town histories for Wales.
Published finding aids: Karen B. Cavanaugh's A Genealogist's
Guide To The Allen County's Public Library (Fort Wayne, n.d.).

66.   INDIANA COMMISSION ON PUBLIC RECORDS
           Archives Division
           Indianapolis, IN.   46204
           (317) 232-1000
       Hours: 8-4:30 M-F.
       Access: Open.
       Copying facilities.
Sources:
Supreme Court Naturalization Records - first papers; index
to naturalization records (records are housed in offices of
clerks of Circuit Court in the 92 counties); Civil War ms.
Published finding aids: None.

67.   INDIANA HISTORICAL SOCIETY LIBRARY
           315 West Ohio Street
           Indianapolis, IN.   46202
           (317) 232-1879
       Hours: 8:30-5 M-F.
       Access: Non-circulating.
       Copying facilities.
Sources:
John Ingle correspondence, 1813-68 (125 items); Thomas Hodg-
son/Thomas Patterson accounts & notes, 1755-1825; John Arnold
notebooks, 1802-15; Richard Hill notebook, 1825-1840 (200
pp.); William Warren Papers, 1841-1859; William Stockdale
Letters, 1865-1910; George Locherbie Letters, 1830-32; John
Walker Descendents, 1749-1914; Joseph Hewitt Letters, 1851-
1872; others.
Published finding aids: None.

68.   INDIANA STATE LIBRARY
           140 N. Senate
           Indianapolis, IN.   46204
           (317) 232-3724
       Hours: 8:15-5 M-F.
       Access: Pre-1900 materials do not circulate.
       Copying facilities.
Sources:
Territorial Court & Executive Records, 1790-1817; records of
Supreme Court of Indiana, 1816-1930; original bills of the
General Assembly, 1863-1957; correspondence of the Governors,
1816-1956; records of Adjutant General's Office, 1803-1921;
Department of Education records, 1844-1935; records of the
State Bank, 1824-70; records of U.S. Land Offices in Indiana,
1805-76; original census schedules for Indiana, 1850-80.
Published finding aids: None.

69.   INDIANA STATE LIBRARY
           Indiana Division
           140 N. Senate Street, Room 210
           Indianapolis, IN.   46204
           (317) 232-3671
       Hours: 8:15-5 M-F.
       Access: Open.
       Copying facilities.
Sources:

3,000,000 items (1778-present), relating chiefly to Indiana
& Midwest, including papers of those who held Federal office
(e.g., Schuyler Colfax, 1878-1926 - 300 items); Oliver H.P.
T. Morton, 1825-77; Daniel D. Pratt, 1832-77 (20,000 items);
Also private persons (e.g. George W. Ewing, 1818-81; Noah
Noble, 1816-44; Lew Wallace, 1861-85); and business records
(account books, letters, & other papers).
Published finding aids: None.

IOWA

70.   IOWA GENEALOGICAL SOCIETY
             6000 Douglas
             Des Moines, IA.   50322
             (515) 276-0287
        Hours: 7-9 T,W,Th.
               1-4 F.
               10-4 Sat.
        Access: Open, but materials do not circulate.
        Copying facilities.
Sources:
Iowa microfilm of census; county histories; vertical file of
family names; some uncatalogued materials.
Published finding aids: I.G.S. Shelf List (1982, 1983).

71.   IOWA STATE DEPARTMENT OF ARCHIVES & HISTORY
             E. 12th Street & Grand Avenue
             Des Moines, IA.   50319
             (515) 281-5472
        Hours: 8-4 M-F.
        Access: Open.
        Copying facilities.
Sources:
L.J. Dickinson Papers (Aldrich, Bradford, Root families);
Joseph H.D. Street Papers (Fitzhugh, Stewart, Grayson); Henry
Summer Papers (Ankeny, Bronson, Fleming, Bradley, Holland);
George Sheppard, 1853 letter with sketch of English Colony;
Scotch-Irish Society clippings.
Published finding aids: None.

72.   IOWA STATE HISTORICAL SOCIETY
             Manuscript Collection
             402 Iowa Avenue
             Iowa City, IA.   52240
             (319) 338-5471
        Hours: 8-4:30 M-F.
        Access: Unrestricted.
        Copying facilities.
Sources:
Newspapers; census rolls (Federal, 1840-1910; State, 1856,
etc.); maps, 1874-1970; manuscripts including Ancient Order
of Hibernians records, 1884-1924; letters from Iowans to

relatives in Ireland, 1848 -; Joseph Tubb Papers, 1844-1927
(letters from England); James Hugh Beed Papers, 1850-1921
(letters to England); Davies/Davis Papers (Welsh in America);
Welsh Congregational Church of Old Man's Creek records, 1846
-1973; William G. Jones Papers; J.R. Williams Papers.
Published finding aids: None.

KANSAS

73.   UNIVERSITY OF KANSAS
            Dept. of Special Collections
            Kenneth Spencer Research Library
            Lawrence, KS.   66045
            (913) 864-4334
        Hours: 8-6 M-F.
        Access: Query before going.
        Copying facilities.
Sources:
James Joyce Collection (900 items); P.S. O'Hegarty Library,
25,000 items on Irish history, 17th-19th century, the Irish
literary renaissance, and Abbey plays and programs; W.B.
Yeats & Yeats Family correspondence (450 items); Irish diaries,
correspondence, journals, and other items.
Published finding aids: A Guide To The Collections (Lawrence,
n.d.), and guides to separate collections.

74.   LEAVENWORTH PUBLIC LIBRARY
            5th & Walnut
            Leavenworth, KS.   66048
            (913) 682-6660
        Hours: 8:30-9 M-Th.
               8:30-5 F-Sat.
        Access: Call ahead.
        Copying facilities.
Sources:
Vertical file of family names; cemetery records & obits.;
church records; old photo albums; marriage records; family
histories (published & unpublished); Federal Census records
(Leavenworth County, 1860-1910); Kansas State Census, 1865-
1925.
Published finding aids: None.

75.   KANSAS STATE HISTORICAL SOCIETY LIBRARY
            120 West 10th
            Topeka, KS.   66612
            (913) 296-2624
        Hours: 9-5 M-F.
        Access: Reference only; materials do not circulate.
        Copying facilities.
Sources:
Socolofsky ms (concerns landlord William Scully, Marion Co.);
Runnymeade Colony ms (Harper County); Victoria Colony ms

(Ellis County); Wakefield Colony (Clay County); Butcher
Family Collection (letters to England, 1871-1890); Pratt
Ranch Collection (Sheridan County); Excelsior Colony (Jewell/
Republic County); Welsh Settlement Papers (Osage, Emporia,
& Riley Counties); Mary Bond ms, 1857 ("First & Second Gener-
ation Irish Immigrants - Patrick and John Kirwan"); Francis
Gerarty Diaries, 1872, 1877; and others.
Published finding aids: None.

76.   WICHITA PUBLIC LIBRARY
              223 South Main
              Wichita, KS   67202
              (316) 262-0611
       Hours: 8:30-9 M-Th.
              8:30-5:30 F-Sat.
              1-5   Sun.
       Access: Reference only.
       Copying facilities.
Sources:
Mostly published items, but the Genealogical Collection contains some 620 individual family histories & some 100 state,
county, and local histories, and the Kansas Reference Collection contains some 430 county and community histories for
Kansas alone, as well as biographical albums and church
histories.
Published finding aids: None.

KENTUCKY

77.   WESTERN KENTUCKY UNIVERSITY
              Dept. of Library Special Collections
              Bowling Green, KY. 42101
              (502) 745-2592 Ext. 11
       Hours: 8-4:30 M-F.
       Access: Unrestricted.
       Copying facilities.
Sources:
Stephens Family Papers (1828, 1842: news of British families,
receipts of William & John Stephens, 1848-85); "The Thomas &
Bridges Story, 1540-1840"; Atkinson Collection (letters from
John and Jane Atkinson to relatives in England, 1866-79, &
more).
Published finding aids: None.

78.   ARCHIVES BRANCH
              Dept. of Library & Archives
              300 Coffee Tree Road/ P.O. Box 537
              Frankfort, KY. 40602
              (502) 875-7000
       Hours: 8-4:30 M-F.
       Access: Varies according to record & agency.
       Copying facilities.
Sources:
Naturalization Proceedings, county by county, 1783-date (be-
fore 1783, see Virginia Archives).
Published finding aids: None.

79.   KENTUCKY DEPT. FOR HUMAN RESOURCES
           Office of Vital Statistics
           275 East Main Street
           Frankfort, KY. 40601
           (502) 564-4530
Sources:
No reply, but birth and death records from 1911.

80.   KENTUCKY HISTORICAL SOCIETY
           Old South Annex, P.O. Box H.
           Frankfort, KY. 40602
           (502) 564-3016
Sources:
Questionnaire not returned.
American Library Directory (50,000 book titles; 8,000 micro-
form; 75,000 maps and photogs; 160 vertical files).

81.   UNIVERSITY OF KENTUCKY
           Margaret I. King Library
           Lexington, KY. 40506-0039
           (606) 257-3801
       Hours: 8-5 M-F.
               8-12 noon Sat.
       Access: Open.
       Copying facilities.
Sources:
Kentucky and Ohio Valley Region records (include social,
business, professional, and personal records; diaries, journals, & oral history; 7,775 microfilm reels of KY county records).
Published finding aids: None.

LOUISIANA

82.   LOUISIANA STATE ARCHIVES & RECORDS
           Office of Secretary of State
           P.O. Box 94125
           Baton Rouge, LA. 70804
           (504) 342-5440
       Hours: 8-4:30 M-F.
       Access: Open.
       Copying facilities.
Sources:
Passenger lists from Customs Service Manifest, Port of New
Orleans, 1813-66; index, 1839-49; passenger lists, vessels
arriving in New Orleans, 1820-1903; Quarterly Abstracts of
vessels arriving in New Orleans (National Archives, MF 272);
New Orleans Citizen and Aliens Manifests (Nat. Arch. MF-T
905); Confederate Pension Applications (give place and date
of birth); voter registrations for 1898 & partial for 1913 -
residence of father and grandfather.
Published finding aids: Handout on genealogical resources
in the State Archives.

83.   LOUISIANA STATE LIBRARY
          760 Riverside Mall
          Baton Rouge, LA.   70821
          (504) 389-6651
      Hours: 8-4:30 M-F.
      Access: Open.
      Copying facilities.
Sources:
Research & related materials for W.P.A. Writers Project
(See Hamer, NUCMC 1959-61).
Published finding aids: None.

84.   LOUISIANA STATE UNIVERSITY
          Dept. of Archives & History
          Baton Rouge, LA.   70803
          (504) 388-2240
      Hours: 7:30-4 M-F.
             8-12 noon Sat.
      Access: Open.
      Copying facilities.
Sources:
Louisiana Materials & Clippings Collection, V.F.; patent
depository; Lower Mississippi Valley Archival Manuscript
Collection, Oral History; U.S. State & UN Documents Dept.
(See NUCMC, 1969-72, & 75).
Published finding aids: None.

85.   HISTORIC NEW ORLEANS COLLECTION
          533 Royal Street
          New Orleans, LA.   70130
          (504) 523-4662
      Hours: 10-4:30 T-Sat.
      Access: Open.
      Copying facilities.
Sources:
Butler Family Papers, 1778-1975 (2,034 items -military,
property, correspondence, & genealogy); Trist Family Papers,
ca. 1625- , ca. 1928 (Trist history including English back-
ground, allied families, notes, letters, & photographs);
Walton-Glenny Family Papers, 1855-1916 (immigrant from Liver-
pool); Martha Gilmore Robinson Collection (191 folders on
Gilmore/Nolan/Maginnis/ & Robinson families).
Published finding aids: None.

86.   NEW ORLEANS PUBLIC LIBRARY
          Louisiana Division
          219 Loyola Avenue
          New Orleans, LA.   70140
          (504) 596-2610
      Hours: 10-6 T-Sat.
      Access: Serious researchers only.
      Copying facilities.
Sources:
Naturalization records, ca. 1827-1906; voter registration
records, ca. 1880-1978; Charity Hospital Admission Books,
1818-1900; New Orleans Newspaper Collection, ca. 1802 -

present; New Orleans City Cemetery records, ca. 1835-1935; also mf of all immigration records for New Orleans, 1820 - 1945.
Published finding aids: C.B. Hamer, Jr. Genealogical Materials in New Orleans Public Library (1975, rev. 1984).

87.   TULANE UNIVERSITY LIBRARY
            Special Collections Division
            Howard-Tilton Memorial Library
            New Orleans, LA.   70118
            (504) 865-5685
        Hours: 8:30-5 M-F.
               9-1   Sat.
        Access: Registration, w/ I.D.
        Copying facilities.
Sources:
Naturalization records of Orleans Parish, 1845-1899, 48 vols.; Papers of Louisiana Historical Association (include family papers, business records, records of organizations, etc.). Published finding aids: None.

MAINE

88.   MAINE BRICK STORE MUSEUM
            117 Main Street
            Kennebunk, ME.   04043
            (207) 985-4802
        Hours: 10-4:30 T-Sat.
        Access: Fee charged.
        Copying facilities.
Sources:
Local histories, primary materials, & genealogical records (Lord, Barry, Thompson, Bourne, & other family names) - mostly 17th century English settlers. Published finding aids: None.

89.   THE KENNEBUNKPORT HISTORICAL SOCIETY
            North Street/ P.O. Box 405
            Kennebunkport, ME.   04046
            (207) 967-2751
        Hours: 2-4:30 T-Th.
        Access: Prior arrangement necessary.
        NO copying facilities.
Sources:
Materials from 1678 (Custom House records, letters, diaries, journals, logbooks, hand-written school books, business records, photographs, & oral history tapes. Published finding aids: None.

90.   ROSE HAWLEY MUSEUM
           305 E. Filer
           Ludington, ME.   49431
           (616) 843-2001
           Hours: 12-5 M-Sat. (June-Aug.)
                  12-5 T, Th. (Other months)
           Access: In-house use only.
           Copying facilities.
Sources:
Local histories, genealogies, diaries, family histories, and
other resources.
Published finding aids: None.

91.   MAINE HISTORICAL SOCIETY
           485 Congress Street
           Portland, ME.   04101
           (207) 774-1822
           Hours: 9-5 T,W,F.
                  9-8:30 Th.
           Access: Open, but restrictions on publication.
           Copying facilities.
Sources:
Everett Schermerhorn Stachpale, "Scotch Exiles in New England"
(1922); E.S. Stachpale, "Character Of The Irish Emigrants
Who Helped To Colonize This State" (n.d.).
Published finding aids: Elizabeth Ring, Reference List of .
Manuscripts Relating to the History of Maine (U. of Maine,
1938).

92.   DYER-YORK LIBRARY & MUSEUM
           371 Main Street
           Saco, ME.   04072
           (207) 283-3861
           Hours: 9-5 M,W,F.
                  1-9 T, Th.
                  9-12 noon Sat.
           Access: Open.
           Copying facilities.
Sources:
(See Hamer: Documents relating to York Co. from 1681-1900 -
census of county, merchants accounts books, and other busi-
ness papers).
Published finding aids: None.

93.   OLD YORK HISTORICAL SOCIETY
           (formerly Old Gaol Museum Library)
           York Street
           Box 188
           York, ME.   03909
           (207) 363-3872
           Access: Non-lending
           Copying facilities.
Sources:
(See Hamer; materials from 1702-1870, include papers of David
Sewall, ships logs & papers, items re: the Old Gaol).
Published finding aids: None.

MARYLAND

94.   MARYLAND DEPARTMENT OF GENERAL SERVICES
            Maryland Hall of Records
            St. John's Street & College Ave./P.O. Box 828
            Annapolis, MD.   21404
            (301) 269-3915
        Hours: 8:30-4:30 M-Sat.
        Access: Open.
        Copying facilities.
Sources:
(NHPRC: Archives of Colony and State of Maryland from 1637;
state, county & local records; personal papers; church his-
tories; business papers; photographs; maps).
Published finding aids: None.

95.   MARYLAND STATE ARCHIVES
            Hall of Records Commission
            Box 828
            Annapolis, MD.   21404
            (301) 269-3914
        Hours: 8:30-4:30 M-Sat.
        Access: Open.
        Copying facilities.
Sources:
Land Patent records 1633-1680; naturalization records, 1658-
1930; miscellaneous records (primarily colonial-era, of
county courts, documenting arrival of convicts & other alien
groups).
Published finding aids: Early Settlers of Maryland: An Index
to Names of Immigrants..., 1633-1680 (Genealogical Publishing
Co., 1974); Colonial Maryland Naturalizations (Genealogical
Publishing Co., 1975).

96.   BALTIMORE CITY ARCHIVES
            211 East Pleasant Street
            Baltimore, MD.   21202
            (302) 396-4863
        Hours: 8:30-4:30 M-F.
        Access: Advance contact needed.
        Copying facilities.
Sources:
Original passenger arrival lists & name index for port of
Baltimore, 1833-66; name-indexed documentation (petitions,
licenses, bonds, muster rolls, correspondence, & reports,
1756-1930); tax records, 1698-present; special 1868 police
census for part of city.
Published finding aids: W.G. LeFurgy's Baltimore Wards, 1797
-1978: A Guide; R.J. Cox's Tracing The History Of The Baltimore Structure.

97.   MARYLAND HISTORICAL SOCIETY
               201 W. Monument Street
               Baltimore, MD.   21201
           (301) 685-3750
           Hours: 11-4:30 T-F.
                   9-4:30 Sat.
           Access: Must apply; adults only.
           Copying facilities.
Sources:
2,600 manuscript collections, mainly 18th to early 20th century, covering the spectrum of MD. history from Calvert Family (MD. colonial proprietors of the 16th c.) to the papers of political and social leaders; business records; civic, religious, literary & social records; published and unpublished literary ms; diaries, accounts, & correspondence; Hibernian Society records, 1816-1978.
Published finding aids: A.J.M. Pedley, MS Collections of the Maryland Historical Society (MHS, 1968); R.J. Cox & L.E. Sullivan, Research Collections of the Maryland Historical Society (MHS, 1981).

98.   MOUNT ST. MARY'S COLLEGE
               Hugh J. Phillips Library
               Emmitsburg, MD.   21727
           (301) 447-6122 Ext. 469
           Hours: 8-4 M-F.
           Access: Prior arrangements necessary.
           Copying facilities.
Sources:
Materials, 1800-present, include journals, papers & letters dealing with Irish Catholicism in Western Maryland.
Published finding aids: None.

99.   MILBOURNE & TULL RESEARCH CENTER
               10605 Lakespring Way
               Hunt Valley, MD.   21030
           (301) 628-2490
           Hours: By appointment.
           Access: By appointment or mail only.
           Copying facilities.
Sources:
Depository for records, research notes & correspondence relating to all Milbourne & Tull families; materials available on other surnames (17th-19th century) for Delaware and Tidewater Md., and Virginia (Adams through Wilson and Wood).
Published finding aids: None.

MASSACHUSETTS

100. ATTLEBORO PUBLIC LIBRARY
          74 North Main Street
          Attleboro, MA. 02703
          (617) 222-0157
      Hours: 9-5:30 M & T.
             1-5:30 W & Th.
             9-5:30 F & Sat.
      Access: Open.
      Copying facilities.
Sources:
Vital records of Attleboro to 1850; data on Coffin, Carpenter,
Holman, Percy, Smith, Small, Shrague, & Stewart families.
Published finding aids: None.

101. BOSTONIAN SOCIETY LIBRARY
          15 State Street
          Boston, MA. 02109
          (617) 242-5614
      Hours:
      Access:
      Copying facilities.
Sources:
(ALD, Hamer, NUCMC, 1959-61 - old maps of Boston; ms from
Volunteer Fire Companies, 1770-1875; volumes relating to
Colonial & Revolutionary period).
Published finding aids: None.

102. HARVARD UNIVERSITY
          Baker Library, Manuscript Dept.
          Soldiers Field Road
          Boston, MA. 02163
          (617) 495-6411
      Hours: 9-5 M-F.
      Access: Open.
      Copying facilities.
Sources:
NHPRC (business records of firms & people engaged in trade
with New England - shipping, textiles, railroads, farming,
storekeeping, & other commercial activities).
Published finding aids: R.W. Lovett & E.C. Bishop, List of
Business MS in Baker Library (1969).

103. MASSACHUSETTS STATE ARCHIVES
          Massachusetts Secretary of State Office
          Room 55, State House
          Boston, MA. 02133
          (617) 727-2816
      Hours: 9-5 M-F.
      Access: Open.
Sources:
Port of Boston passenger lists, 1848-1891; vital records
(births, deaths, marriages), 1841-1890; Federal Census schedules, 1790-1880; State Census schedules, 1855, 1865.

Published finding aids: <u>Surname Index to Passenger Lists</u>
<u>(1848-91)</u> on MF from National Archives; <u>Surname Index to</u>
<u>Vital Records on MF</u> through Latter Day Saints Church.

104. MASSACHUSETTS STATE HISTORICAL SOCIETY
            1154 Boylston Street
            Boston, MA.   02215
            (617) 536-1608
Questionnaire not returned; See Hamer & G.K. Hall Catalogue
of MSHS holdings.

105. MASSACHUSETTS STATE LIBRARY
            341 State House
            Boston, MA.   02133
            (617) 727-2590
        Hours: 9-5 M-F.
        Access: Open.
        Copying facilities.
Sources:
NHPRC, Hamer, NUCMC, 1967-68. (Legislative & Executive docu-
ments, Colonial period to the 1930's, and related materials).

106.   NEW ENGLAND HISTORIC GENEALOGICAL SOCIETY
            101 Newbury Street
            Boston, MA.   02116
            (617) 536-5740
        Hours: 9-4:45 T-Sat.
        Access: Fee for non-members.
        Copying facilities.
Sources:
Over 5,000 shelf feet of manuscript items relating to New
England families & their descendents & the Colonial period.
(See next NUCMC for 100+ entries). Family materials include
Walter E. Corbin's Vital Records of Many Towns in Central
& Western Massachusetts; Fred E. Crowell's New Englanders in
Nova Scotia; Mrs. Winifred Lovering Holman Dodge's Genealogy
of over 12,000 American families; George A. Moriarty's Collec-
tion of English-American Genealogy; and studies by several
others.
Published finding aids: None.

107.   HOUGHTON LIBRARY - HARVARD UNIVERSITY
            Rare Books & Manuscripts
            Cambridge, MA.   02138
            (617) 495-2441
        Hours: 9-5 M-F.
        Access: Open.
        Copying facilities.
Sources:
Hamer (British Papers, 1758 - ; Canadiana, 1599-1822; papers
of presidents & others in federal government; papers of his-
torians, clergymen, philosophers, & authors; archives of
American Board of Commissioners for Foreign Missions, 1812-1945)
Published finding aids: Annual Houghton Library <u>Report of</u>
<u>Accessions</u> (since 1941-42).

108.   DEDHAM HISTORICAL SOCIETY
            612 High Street, P.O. Box 215
            Dedham, MA. 02026
            (641) 326-1385
        Hours: 1-5 T-F.
                Or by appointment.
        Access: Generally unrestricted.
        Copying facilities.
Sources:
MS from 1638-1954, include Fisher Ames Papers, 1775-1808;
Horace Mann Papers, 1832-52; records of various societies &
associations, 1802-70; diary of Samuel Dexter, 1722-52; church
records (Congregational & Episcopal), 1638-1890.
Published finding aids: None.

109.   HARVARD PUBLIC LIBRARY
            Harvard Common
            Harvard, MA. 01451
            (617) 456-3678
        Hours: 10-9 T, Th.
               10-6 W, F.
               10-4 Sat.
        Access: Open.
        Copying facilities.
Sources:
Hapgood Family; Nourse's History of Harvard.
Published finding aids: None.

110.   HAVERHILL PUBLIC LIBRARY
            99 Main Street
            Haverhill, MA. 01830
            (617) 373-1586
        Hours: 1-9 M-W.
               9-5:30 Sat.
        Access: Closed stacks.
        Copying facilities.
Sources:
Alfred Poor ms, 1851 (gives genealogical background of all
inhabitants of town of Groveland, East Parish of Bradford,
MA. until 1850; Irish mill operations gave birthplace &
parents' names).
Published finding aids: None.

111.   LANCASTER TOWN LIBRARY
            Main Street
            Lancaster, MA. 01523
            (617) 365-2008
        Hours: 10-8 T-Th.
               10-5 F.
               2-5 Sat.
        Access: By appointment only.
        Copying facilities.
Sources:
Henry S. Nource MS Collection (ms relating to Lancaster, 1644
-1800, "Historical & Genealogical Sketches of Earliest Pioneers in Lancaster"); F.L. Weiss's "Early Families of Lan-

caster...1643-1700".
Published finding aids: H.S. Nource <u>Early Records of Lan-</u>
<u>caster, 1643-1725</u> (1884); <u>Lancastriana I: A Supplement</u> (1900),
& <u>Lancastriana II: A Bibliography</u> (1901).

112.   LYNN HISTORICAL SOCIETY
    125 Green Street
    Lynn, MA. 01902
    (617) 592-2465
   Hours: 9-4 M-F.
     1-4 Sat.
   Access: Non-circulating.
   Copying facilities.
Sources:
Miscellaneous ms (genealogies, family & local histories,
scrapbooks); vital records; city directories.
Published finding aids: None.

113.   MARBLEHEAD HISTORICAL SOCIETY
    161 Washington Street, P.O. Box 1048
    Marblehead, MA. 01945
    (617) 631-1439
   Hours: 9:30-4 M-Sat.
   Access: Open; non-circulating.
   Copying facilities.
Sources:
Genealogical materials on Marblehead families; letters, deeds,
bills, & other family records; records of military involve-
ment; records of schools & other organizations.
Published finding aids: In preparation (Thomas Gray).

114.   NEWBURYPORT PUBLIC LIBRARY
    94 State Street
    Newburyport, MA. 01950
    (617) 462-4031
   Hours: 9-5 T-Sat.
   Access: Open; non-circulating.
   Copying facilities.
Sources:
Pamphlets, photos, maps, broadsides, local genealogies.
Published finding aids: None.

115.   ESSEX INSTITUTE
    132 Essex Street
    Salem, MA. 01970
    (617) 744-3390
   Hours: 9-4:30 M-F.
   Access: Fee for non-members; closed stacks.
   Copying facilities.
Sources:
Ship Australia, logbook 1851, New York to New Orleans and
Liverpool, including passenger list (English & Irish immi-
grants from Liverpool).
Published finding aids: None.

116. GOODNOW LIBRARY
            21 Concord Road
            Sudbury, MA. 01776
            (617) 443-9112
        Hours: 9-9 M-W.
               9-5 Th.-Sat.
        Access: On-site use only.
        Copying facilities.
Sources:
MF of Sudbury Town & Church Records from 1638 - : extensive
but printed family & local history collections.
Published finding aids: "Selection of Genealogical & Histori-
cal Materials in the Goodnow Library" (pamphlet, n.d.).

117. SWANSEA PUBLIC LIBRARY
            69 Main Street
            Swansea, MA. 02777
            (617) 674-9609
        Hours: 10-5 M-F.
               1:30-5 Sat.
        Access: Open; non-circulating.
        Copying facilities.
Sources:
Materials relating to Swansea & its residents; 17th century
deeds & other records; logbooks of voyages; photographs; ms;
maps; oral history tapes.
Published finding aids: None.

118. OLD COLONY HISTORICAL SOCIETY
            66 Church Green
            Taunton, MA. 02780
            (617) 822-1622
        Hours: 10-4 T-Sat.
        Access: Open; appointment helpful.
        Copying facilities.
Sources:
Collection consists of wills, deeds, diaries, account books,
journals, business records, and other historical items re-
lating to the Old Colony.
Published finding aids: None.

119. FEDERAL ARCHIVES & RECORDS CENTER
            c/o Regional Archivist
            380 Trapelo Road
            Waltham, MA. 02154
            (617) 647-8100
        Hours: 8-4:30 M-F.
        Access: Most collections open.
        Copying facilities.
Sources:
(Serves CT., MA., ME., N.H., R.I., & VT.). Records of District Courts of U.S. (Civil, Criminal, Admiralty, & Bankruptcy), 1789 to present; Records of United Courts of Appeals,
1789 to present; Records of Bureau of Indian Affairs; Records
of Bureau of Customs; Records of Office of the Chief of
Engineers; census records; NARC microfilms (genealogy/ethnolo-

gy).
Published finding aids: <u>Research Opportunities</u> (General
Services Administration: National Archives & Records Services,
1980).

120. WENHAM PUBLIC LIBRARY
          Main Street
          Wenham, MA. 01984
          (617) 468-4062
          Hours: 10-5 M-F.
          Access: In-house use.
          Copying facilities.
Sources:
Vital statistics to 1850; town histories; Wenham town records,
1642-on; Salem town records, 1634-91; family genealogies
(Dodge, Gove, Kimball, Knowlton, Moulton, White, & Wilkins).
Published finding aids: None.

121. WESTBOROUGH PUBLIC LIBRARY
          55 West Main Street
          Westborough, MA.
          (617) 366-0725
          Hours: 10-6 M,W,F.
                 10-9 T,Th.
                 10-5 Sat.
Sources:
Church records & diaries of Ebenezer Parkman, minister in
Westborough from 1724-1782.
Published finding aids: None.

122. AMERICAN ANTIQUARIAN SOCIETY
          185 Salisbury Street
          Worcester, MA. 01609
          (617) 755-5221
          Hours: 9-5 M-F.
          Access: Open to qualified adults with reference letters
                  & two forms of identification; interview ne-
                  cessary.
          Copying facilities.
Sources:
Boston, Mass. Papers, 1634-1893; some tax & census records,
1657-1795; Daniel Fisher Papers, 1790-1837 (Irish emigree,
1797); Susan E. Parsons Brown Forbes Diaries, 1841-1908
(Alexander Barclay Forbes, a Scottish immigrant, used Irish
immigrants as servants); Lambert Family Papers, 1821-1887
(English family emigrated to America in 1820's); New England
Council Records, 1622-1623; Paine Family Papers, c. 1721-
c. 1918; Caroline Barrett White Diaries, 1849-1914 (relations
with Irish servants); Worcester, MA. families, Genealogy
Notes; Worcester, MA. Papers, 1665-c. 1954 (includes some tax
& census records); local census records.
Published finding aids: <u>Catalogue of the MS Collections of
the American Antiquarian Society</u> (G.K. Hall, 1979).

MICHIGAN

123.   BENTLEY HISTORICAL LIBRARY
            Michigan Historical Collection
            1150 Beal Avenue
            Ann Arbor, MI.   48109-2113
            (313) 764-3482
        Hours: 8:30-5 M-F.
        Access: Open.
        Copying facilities.
Sources:
Jane Trattles Letters, 1854-68, to England; Charles Foster
Diary, 1836-1839; Birney, McClear, Hanherd Family Papers,
1839-1949; Letters of the McVea Family, 1899-1926; Monaghan
Family Papers, 1851-1883, & 1949-1976; Records of St. Anne
Parish, Detroit, 1704-1844; Tuomy Papers, 1870-1947.
Published finding aids: F.X. Blouin & R.M. Warner's Sources
For The Study Of Migration & Ethnicity (Ann Arbor: Bentley
Historical Library, 1979).

124.   UNIVERSITY OF MICHIGAN
            Ann Arbor, MI.   48109
(See Bentley Historical Library above).

125.   BURTON HISTORICAL COLLECTION - DETROIT PUBLIC LIBRARY
            Detroit, MI.   48202
            (313) 833-1480 or 833-1481
        Hours: 9:30-5:30 T,Th., F., & Sat.
            1-9   W.
        Access: Open.
        Copying facilities.
Sources:
Richard R. Elliott Papers, 1848-80 (12 volumes of letterbooks,
Elliott acting as agent to bring Irish immigrants to Michi-
gan; includes immigration register for 1851-69).
Published finding aids: None.

126.   SACRED HEART SEMINARY LIBRARY
            2701 Chicago Blvd.
            Detroit, MI.   48206
            (313) 868-2700
        Hours: 9-9 M-F.
            12-5 Sat.-Sun.
        Access: Open.
        Copying facilities.
Sources:
Manuscripts from 1800 include Catholic Church records from
Davison & Detroit, 1836 - ; Parish History Collection, 1880
- ; receipt book, 1840-48; The Angelus, 1884-96, newspaper;
The Gabriel Richard Collection, ca. 1850 (Detroit Catholic
Temperance Society - membership list & contributions).
Published finding aids: None.

127. MICHIGAN STATE UNIVERSITY
        Archives & Special Collections
        East Lansing, MI. 48824
        (517) 355-2330
        Hours: 8-5 M-F.
        Access: Open.
        Copying facilities.
Sources:
Manuscripts from 1713 include historical materials on Michigan, families, businesses, and other organizations; 40 groups
of Civil War Letters; McIntosh Blacksmith Shop records, 1883
-1917 (ledgers and journals); Charles Hutchinson Thompson
Papers, 1843-1916 (journals, diaries, genealogy & correspondence); Harold Smith Patton Papers, 1915-1941 (journal &
correspondence).
Published finding aids: Honart, Pyzik, & Howard's Guide To
The Michigan State University Archives... (1976).

128. GRAND RAPIDS PUBLIC LIBRARY
        60 Library Plaza
        Grand Rapids, MI. 49503
        (616) 456-4424
        Hours: 12-9 T-W.
               9-5:30 Th.-Sat.
        Access: Open.
        Copying facilities.
Sources:
MS identify immigrants from New England (Ball Letters, Camp-
bell Letters, Rebecca Richmond Letters & Diaries, William
Almy Richmond Letters, John W. Squirer Letters); Federal
Census for Michigan & Indexes for 23 states.
Published finding aids: "Grand Rapids Public Library, Michi-
gan & Family History Department" (typescript, n.d.).

129. HERRICH PUBLIC LIBRARY
        300 River Avenue
        Holland, MI. 49423
        (616) 392-3114
        Hours: 9-9 M-F.
               9-6 Sat.
               2-5 Sun.
        Access: User fee for non-residents.
        Copying facilities.
Sources:
Materials from 1840, local & family history of the Holland
area; indexes to the Genealogical Surname Collection by
Grace C. Keeler ("Upham Records, Book One"; "More Uphams";
"Upham Allied Lines"; "Burson Family of Schoolcraft"; "Briggs
Research"; "Ancestry of Max Bement"; "The Beals Family";
"The Family of Barher").
Published finding aids: Genealogy...Materials Available at
Herrich Public Library (Pamphlet, 1980).

130. MICHIGAN STATE ARCHIVES
            3405 North Logan
            Lansing, MI. 48918
            (517) 373-0512
        Hours: 8-5 M-F.
        Access: Open.
        Copying facilities.
Sources:
Manuscripts from 1810 include state government records,
county, city, & township records (tax assessment rolls);
Federal Census schedules; State Census schedules; military
records; Civil War Graves registration; photograph files.
(See Michigan State Library, 735 East Michigan Ave., for
published materials).
Published finding aids: 20 for archival materials; 5 for
maps & photographs; 2 for non-governmental collections.

131. MARQUETTE COUNTY HISTORICAL SOCIETY
            213 North Front Street
            Marquette. MI. 49855
        Sources:
Questionnaire not returned. (See Hamer, NUCMC, 1959-61; F.X.
Blouin & R.M. Warner's Sources For The Study Of Migration &
Ethnicity, Ann Arbor: Bentley Historical Library, 1979).
132. SANILAC COUNTY HISTORICAL SOCIETY MUSEUM
            Port Sanilac, MI.
        Sources:
Blouin & Warner (John Jones Journal, 1890; Loop-Harrison
Family Records, McGregor-McLeod Family Papers, McGregor-
Thayer Family Diary).

MINNESOTA

133. FREEBORN COUNTY HISTORICAL SOCIETY
            Freeborn County Fairgrounds
            North Bridge/ Box 105
            Albert Lea, MN. 56007
            (507) 373-8003
        Hours: 1-5 T., Th., & Sun.
        Access: Prior arrangement required.
        Copying facilities.
Sources:
NHPRC (Materials from 1849 include diaries, manuscripts, &
genealogies for Freeborn and surrounding counties).
Published finding aids: None.

134. ANOKA COUNTY HISTORICAL/GENEALOGICAL SOCIETY
            1900 3rd Avenue South
            Anoka, MN. 55303
            (612) 421-0600
        Hours: 12:30-4 T-F.
        Access: On-premise use only.
        Copying facilities.

Sources:
Anoka County records & newspapers, 1863-1920; cemetery inscriptions, church records, surname index system.
Published finding aids: None.

135. BEMIDJI STATE UNIVERSITY
          A.C. Clark Library
          Bemidji, MN. 56601
          (218) 755-2955
      Hours: 8-4:30 M-F.
      Access: Open.
      Copying facilities.
Sources:
North Central Minnesota Historical Center Collection
(affiliate of the Minn. Hist. Society)includes ms & oral
history tapes; Not indexed.
Published finding aids: None.

136. ST. LOUIS COUNTY HISTORICAL SOCIETY
          506 West Michigan Street
          Duluth, MN. 55802
          (218) 722-8011
      Hours: 9-5 M-F.
      Access: Permission needed.
      NO copying facilities.
Sources:
NHPRC (Materials, from 1679, include diaries of missionaries
and pioneers; materials relating to the fur trade, mining,
shipping, and settlement; records of the Great Lakes - Tidewater Association).
Published finding aids: None.

137. SOUTHWEST STATE UNIVERSITY
          Southwest Minnesota Historical Center
          Marshall, MN. 56258
          (507) 537-7373
      Hours: 9-4 M-F.
             Sat. & Sun. by appointment.
      Access: Open.
      Copying facilities.
Sources:
NHPRC (Materials, from 1860, include diaries, correspondence,
legislator's papers, church records, records of farm organizations; collection is focused on the 17 counties of southwest
Minnesota).
Published finding aids: None.

138. MINNEAPOLIS PUBLIC LIBRARY & INFORMATION CENTER
          Minneapolis Historical Collection
          300 Nicallet Mall
          Minneapolis, MN. 55401
          (612) 372-6648
      Hours: 9-5:30 M-F.
             9:30-5:30 Sat.
      Access: Adults only.
      Copying facilities.

Sources:
NHPRC (Materials, from 1851, include family papers, women's
club papers, correspondence, and scrapbooks).
Published finding aids: None.

139.   BROWN COUNTY HISTORICAL SOCIETY
          27 North Broadway
          New Ulm, MN. 56073
          (507) 354-2016
       Hours: 1-5 M-F.
       Access: Query first.
       Copying facilities.
Sources:
(See Hamer, NHPRC): Materials, from 1854, include collections
on the pioneers & their families, 1855-1960 (9,000+ pieces);
Brown County Records, 1857-1960; New Ulm, 1855-1960, records;
Land Company records, 1854-59; military history, 1861-1945;
autographed letters & photographs, 1890-1925.
Published finding aids: None.

140.   COLLEGE OF ST. THOMAS
          O'Shaughnessy Library
          Celtic Collection
          St. Paul, MN. 55105
          (612) 647-5796 or 5726
       Hours: 12:30-4:30 F.
             Or by appointment.
       Access: Query first.
       Copying facilities.
Sources:
Depository for St. Andrews Society of Minnesota Records;
published histories of many towns, counties, & villages with
Celtic connections.
Published finding aids: None.

141.   MINNESOTA HISTORICAL SOCIETY
          Division of Archives & Manuscripts
          1500 Mississippi Street
          St. Paul, MN. 55101
          (612) 296-6980
       Hours: 8:30-5 M-F.
       Access: Approval necessary.
       Copying facilities.
Sources:
Collection includes The Minnesota State Archives (30,000 ft.
of material ranging from naturalization records for 75 of the
87 counties to letters of governors) and records (15,000) of
Great Northern & Northern Pacific Railway companies (includes
records of land departments and immigration data); W.P.A.
Papers, 1849-1942; Presbyterian Church records; Family names
of all four immigrant groups in letters, diaries, family
histories; Irish-American Colonization Papers, 1872-1909;
Patrick Henry Rahilly Papers, 1874-1930; Ignatius Donnelly
Papers.
Published finding aids: 15.

MISSISSIPPI

142. MISSISSIPPI DEPARTMENT OF ARCHIVES & HISTORY
          P.O. Box 571
          100 S. State Street
          Jackson, MS. 39205-0571
          (601) 354-6218
      Hours: 8-5 M-F.
             8:30-4:30 Sat.
      Access: Open.
      Copying facilities.
Sources:
Hamer, NHPRC, NUCMC, 1959-62, 69-70. (Materials, from 1699,
include records of land titles; records of French, Spanish,
& British administrations of Miss. territory; records of the
territory; records of the state & county; records of organizations, individuals, businesses, & churches; includes 2,000
private collections.
Published finding aids: <u>Manuscript Collection Title List</u>
(5/14/84).

143. UNIVERSITY OF MISSISSIPPI LIBRARY
          Archives & Special Collections
          University, MS. 38677
          (601) 232-7408
      Hours: 8:30-8 M-Th.
             8:30-5 F.
             9-12 noon Sat.
      Access: Open.
      Copying facilities.
Sources:
NHPRC & Hamer (Manuscripts, from 1800, include materials on
the lumber industry, the University, and political figures).
Published finding aids: None.

MISSOURI

144. UNIVERSITY OF MISSOURI AT COLUMBIA
          23 Ellis Library
          Columbia, MO. 65201
          (314) 882-6028
      Hours: 8-4:45 M-F.
      Access: Open, but permission needed to duplicate some
              items.
      Copying facilities.
Sources:
State Historical Society of Missouri ms and w/ U. of MO. at
St. Louis, the Western Historical Manuscript Collection.
Collection includes Abdiel Leonard Papers, 1769-1928 (deeds,
legal cases, bills, receipts, & military correspondence);
Ozark Land & Lumber Company Papers, 1887-1933; Brinkerhoft

& Smith Land Agency & Loan; Charles W. Clark Papers, 1854-1911; W.C. Breckenridge Papers, 1752-1927; C.E. Breckenridge Papers, 1897-1960; Missouri State Archives, 1806-1957; Macfarlane Family Letters, 1828-44; Bernard F. Dickinson Papers, 1900-1971; and Colonel Joseph Crochett's Genealogy.
Published finding aids: In preparation.

145. MISSOURI STATE RECORDS & ARCHIVES
                Adjutant General of Missouri
                1717 Industrial Drive
                Jefferson City, MO. 65101
                (314) 751-2321
        Hours: 8-5 M-F.
        Access: Open.
        NO copying facilities.
Sources:
NHPRC (Military records of citizens of the state for all wars, foreign & domestic, since 1812).
Published finding aids: None.

146. FEDERAL ARCHIVES & RECORDS CENTER
                c/o Regional Archivist
                2306 East Bannister Road
                Kansas City, MO. 64131
                (816) 926-7271
        Hours: 8-4 M-F.
        Access: Most collections open.
        Copying facilities.
Sources:
(Serves IA., KN., MO., & NE.). Records of District Courts of U.S. (Civil, Criminal, Admiralty, & Bankruptcy) until the 1950's; Records of United Courts of Appeals, 1891-1950's; Records of Bureau of Indian Affairs; Records of Bureau of Customs; Records of Office of the Chief of Engineers; census records; NARC Microfilms (genealogy/ ethnology).
Published finding aids: Research Opportunities (General Services Administration: National Archives and Records Service 1980).

147. MISSOURI HISTORICAL SOCIETY ARCHIVES
                Jefferson Memorial Building
                Lindell Blvd. at DeBaliviere
                St. Louis, MO. 63112
                (314) 361-1424
        Hours: 9:30-4:30 T-Sat.
        Access: Fee for non-members.
        Copying facilities.
Sources:
NHPRC, Hamer, NUCMC, 1962-68, 70, 73, 76 (Manuscripts, from 1664, focus on the West, the history of Missouri, & St. Louis; include tax, census, & court records of colonial capitals of New Madrid, St. Charles, & St. Louis; cover fur trade, mititary exploration, frontier, & business).
Published finding aids: None.

148.   ST. LOUIS PUBLIC LIBRARY
            History & Genealogy Department
            1301 Olive Street
            St. Louis, MO.   63103
            (314) 241-2288
         Hours: 9-9 M.
                9-5 T-Sat.
         Access: Adults.
         Copying facilities.
Sources:
Microforms of Federal Census (all states, many issues); military records; passenger lists & indexes; and some Eastern
newspapers; about 3,000 completed family histories; card
files for genealogy & local history.
Published finding aids: Georgia Gambrill, Genealogical
Materials & Local Histories in the St. Louis Public Library
(rev. ed., 1966); First Supplement (1971).

149.   UNIVERSITY OF MISSOURI AT ST. LOUIS
            8001 Natural Bridge
            St. Louis, MO.   63121
            (314) 241-2288
         Hours: 9-9 M.
                9-5 T-Sat.
         Access: Adults.
         Copying facilities.
Sources:
(w/ U. of Missouri at Columbia) Joint Collection, Western
Historical Manuscript Collection (see #144); other ms
include Mary Margaret Ellis Memoirs, 1914-1930; Fellowship
of America's Loyal Irish Record Book, 1929-30; John Nooney
Papers, 1882-1939; Handley-Taylor Papers, 1809-1945; 16 oral
history tapes.
Published finding aids: In preparation.

MONTANA

150.   MONTANA STATE UNIVERSITY
            Special Collections
            Bozeman, MT.   59715
            (406) 994-4242
         Hours: 8-12 & 1-5 M-F.
         Access: Supervised.
         Copying facilities.
Sources:
Materials relate to the history of Montana, the Western Move-
ment, and Yellowstone National Park; include diaries and
correspondence files.
Published finding aids: None, but refer to Cockhill & John-
son's Guide to Manuscripts in Montana Repositories (U. of
Montana Libraries, 1973).

151. MONTANA HISTORICAL SOCIETY ARCHIVES
             225 North Roberts Street
             Helena, MT. 59620-9990
             (406) 444-4774
      Hours: 8-5 M-F.
             9-5 Sat. (Sept. - May)
      Access: Open.
      Copying facilities.
Sources:
Collections include papers of individuals (Bumby, Cruse,
Dawson, Duane, Hogan, Jeenings, Kelly, Tweet, & others);
records of businesses owned by British companies (e.g.,
Hudson Bay Co., 1854-56; Montana Mining, 1887-93; New Mine
Saphire Syndicate, 1898-1958); genealogical sources such as
Benton Ave. Cemetery Association, 1909-1922, Virginia City
Episcopal Church, 1867-1919, & Jefferson County records,
1865-85; and general sources on immigration & ethnic groups.
Published finding aids: Cockhill & Johnson's Guide to Manu-
scripts in Montana Repositories (U. of Montana Libraries,
1973).

152. UNIVERSITY OF MONTANA LIBRARY
             Missoula, MT. 59812
             (406) 243-2053
      Hours: 8-5 M-F.
      Access: Open.
      Copying facilities.
Sources:
Materials, from 1860, include archives of the University &
records relating to business, political, and social history
of the state.
Pulbished finding aids: Refer to Cockhill & Johnson, above.

NEBRASKA

153. NORTH PLATTE VALLEY HISTORICAL ASSOCIATION
             11th & J. Streets, Oregon Trail Park
             Gering, NE. 69341
             (308) 436-5411
      Hours: 8-5 M-F.
             1-5 Sun.
      Access: Open.
      Copying facilities.
Sources:
NHPRC (Materials, from 1887, include diaries, letters, club
minutes, & other items relating to the North Platte Valley).
Published finding aids: None.

154. NEBRASKA STATE HISTORICAL SOCIETY
          State Archives Division
          1500 R. Street / P.O. Box 82554
          Lincoln, NE. 68501
          (402) 432-2793
      Hours: 8-5 M-Sat.
      Access: Open, but registration required.
      Copying facilities.
Sources:
Donald F. Danker Collection of Family Folders (Tighe & Casey,
Dougherty, Orr, Jones, Mullin, Fritton, & Fox, Gibbons, &
Murphy); Ancient Order of Hibernians of Lincoln Papers; Post-
ville Welsh Church Records; Rosefield Sabbath School & Church
Records (Trenton, Neb.).
Published finding aids: Guide to the MS Division (1974), &
Guide to the MS Division (1983).

155. OMAHA PUBLIC LIBRARY
          215 South 15th Street
          Omaha, NE. 68102-1004
          (402) 444-4800
Sources:
See: Hamer, NUCMC, 1962, ALD.
Questionnaire not returned.

156. UNION PACIFIC HISTORICAL MUSEUM
          1416 Dodge Street
          Omaha, NE. 68179
          (402) 271-3530
      Hours: 9-5 M-F.
             9-1 Sat.
      Access: Restricted to serious scholars.
      Copying facilities.
Sources:
Hamer, NHPRC (Materials, from 1900, include Union Pacific
Railroad Records and numerous photographs and slides relating
to railroads, the West, and Midwest).
Published finding aids: None.

NEVADA

157. NEVADA STATE DIVISION OF ARCHIVES & RECORDS
          101 S. Fall Street, Capitol Complex
          Carson City, NV. 89710
          (702) 885-5210
      Hours: 8-12 & 1-5 M-F.
      Access: Open, but some materials restricted.
      Copying facilities.
Sources:
Collections, from 1857, include state, county, and city government archives, materials relating to government officials
& employees, military records, copies of U.S. Censuses.

Published finding aids: None.

158. LAS VEGAS BRANCH GENEALOGICAL LIBRARY
         P.O. Box 1360
         Las Vegas, NV. 89125
         (702) 382-9695
      Hours: 9-5 M.
             9-9 T-F.
      Access: Open.
      Copying facilities.
Sources:
Microfilm & microfiche collection of Federal Censuses, pass-
enger lists, and other genealogical materials; some pamphlets
and ms.
Published finding aids: None.

159. NEVADA HISTORICAL SOCIETY
         1665 N. Virginia
         Reno, NV. 89507
         (702) 784-6397 or 6398
      Hours: 8-5 M-F.
             9-5 Sat. & Sun.
      Access: Open.
      Copying facilities.
Sources:
Hamer, NHPRC (Materials, from 1846, include pioneer diaries,
reminiscences, some territorial and state records, complete
records of Episcopal Diocese of Nevada, records of business
groups, and personal papers of prominent citizens).
Published finding aids: None.

160. NEVADA STATE GENEALOGICAL SOCIETY
         P.O. Box 20666
         Reno, NV. 89515
Questionnaire not returned. Not in Hamer, NHPRC.

NEW HAMPSHIRE

161. NEW HAMPSHIRE BUREAU OF VITAL RECORDS
         Health & Welfare Building
         Hazen Drive
         Concord, N.H. 03301
         (603) 271-4650
      Hours: 8:30-4 M-F.
      Access: Open.
Sources:
Births (prior to 1901), death, marriage and divorce records
prior to 1938.
Published finding aids: None.

162.   NEW HAMPSHIRE DIVISION OF RECORDS MANAGEMENT/RECORDS
          71 South Fruit Street
          Concord, N.H.   03301
          (603) 271-2236
       Hours: 8-4:30 M-F.
       Access: Few restrictions.
       Copying facilities.
Sources:
Census records for 1732, 1776, & 1880; Town Inventories;
town records; deeds & probate records; military records;
Name Change Index & Laws.
Published finding aids: <u>Guide to Early Documents (c. 1680 -
c. 1900) at the New Hampshire Records Management & Archives
Center</u> (1981).

163.   NEW HAMPSHIRE HISTORICAL SOCIETY
          30 Park Street
          Concord, N.H.   03301
          (603) 225-3381
       Hours: 9-4:30 M-Sat.
       Access: Open.
       Copying facilities.
Sources:
New England and New Hampshire materials, from 1623, include
local histories, papers, diaries, town records, account
books, shipping records, minutes of social organizations,
school and church records; Abbott-Downing Company Records;
thousands of genealogies.
Published finding aids: None.

164.   NEW HAMPSHIRE STATE LIBRARY
          20 Park Street/ Box 189
          Concord, N.H.   03301
Hamer, NUCMC, 1966 (has U.S. Censuses for N.H., 1790-1910).
1910).

165.   PORTSMOUTH ATHENAEUM
          9 Market Square
          Portsmouth, N.H.   03801-0848
          (603) 431-2538
       Hours: 1-4 Th. & by appointment.
       Access: Query first.
       Copying facilities.
Sources:
Pamphlet files with church histories, city histories & guides,
city directories; published volumes include U.S. Customs
records; historical and genealogical registers; and family
genealogies.
Published finding aids: None.

NEW JERSEY

166. FEDERAL ARCHIVES & RECORDS CENTER
          c/o Regional Archivist
          Building 22 - Military Ocean Terminal Bayonne
          Bayonne, N.J.   07002
          (201) 823-7251
      Hours: 8-4 M-F.
      Access: Most collections open.
      Copying facilities.
Sources:
(Serves N.J., N.Y., P.R., & V.I.); Records of District Courts
of U.S. (Civil, Criminal, Admiralty, & Bankruptcy) until the
1950's; Records of United Courts of Appeals, 1891-1950's;
Records of Bureau of Indian Affairs; Records of Bureau of
Customs; Records of Office of the Chief of Engineers; NARC
microfilms (genealogy/ethnology).
Published finding aids: Research Opportunities (General
Services Administration: National Archives & Records Service,
1980).

167. DELIA BIDDLE PUGH LIBRARY
          Burlington County Historical Society
          457 High Street
          Burlington, N.J.   08016
          (609) 386-4773
      Hours: 1-4 W.
             10-12 noon Th-F.
             2-4 Sun., & by appointment.
      Access: By permission.
      Copying facilities.
Sources:
Deeds, photographs, maps, brochures, pamphlets, Bible records,
family trees, miscellaneous family notes; Atsion record books;
Abolition Society Papers; James Fenimore Cooper Collection.
Published finding aids: None.

168. NEW JERSEY SOCIETY, S.A.R.
          1045 East Jersey Street
          Elizabeth, N.J.   07201
          (201) 355-1776
      Hours: 9-4 T & Th.
      Access: Must write first.
      Copying facilities.
Sources:
6,400 applications of S.A.R. members, 1899-present (some list
place of birth of veteran, some are from the British Isles).
Published finding aids: None.

169. HUNTERDON COUNTY HISTORICAL SOCIETY
          114 Main Street
          Flemington, N.J.   08822
          (201) 782-1091
      Hours: 1-3 Th. & Sat. & by appointment.
      Access: By permission.

Copying facilities.
Sources:
Capner/Capnerhurst Family Papers, 1776-1846 (financial re-
cords, documents, & correspondence of the family, friends,
& relatives).
Published finding aids: None.

170. MONMOUTH COUNTY HISTORICAL ASSOCIATION
            70 Court Street
            Freehold, N.J.   07728
            (201) 462-1466
        Hours: 10-4 W-Sat.
        Access: Open.
        Copying facilities.
Sources:
Shanck Family Papers, 1741-1906 (financial records, legal
records, & estate papers; genealogical charts); Hartshorne
Family Papers, 1771-1954 & 1664-1915 (records of Hartshorne,
Stabler, & other connections); Louise Hartshorne Collection,
1778-1953 (Conover, Hartshorne, Henderson); Cherry Hall Papers
1682-1941 (Brown, Brearly, Holmes, Johnson, Motl, Rhea, etc);
Conover Family Papers, 1700-1897 (deeds, wills, cash accounts
& loan books).
Published finding aids: Guide to Genealogical Resources in
the Monmouth County Historical Association Library (n.d.).

171. UNITED METHODIST CHURCH
            Archives & History Center
            P.O. Box 127
            Madison, N.J.   07940
            (201) 822-2787
        Hours: 9-5 M-F.
        Access: Some materials restricted.
Sources:
Obituary file and other data for Methodist/United Methodist
ministers, 1773-present.
Published finding aids: None.

172. MORRISTOWN & MORRIS TOWNSHIP
            Joint Free Public Library
            1 Miller Road
            Morristown, N.J.   07960
            (201) 538-6161
        Hours: 9-9 M-F.
            9:30-5 Sat.
            1-5 Sun.
        Access: Open.
        Copying facilities.
Sources:
Census records, city directories, military & pension re-
cords, church & cemetery records, town & county records,
deeds & legal titles, school records, club records, diaries
& journals, account books, family papers (Cutler, DeCamp,
Dixon, Howell, Sharp).
Published finding aids: Guide to New Jersey MS in Morris
County (NJHC, c. 1983).

173. NEW JERSEY HISTORICAL SOCIETY
              230 Broadway
              Newark, N.J.   07104
              (201) 483-3939
       Hours: 9:30-4:15 M-Sat.
       Access: Open; appointments preferred.
       Copying facilities.
Sources:
Scott Family Papers, 1792-1865 (include letters to relatives
in England); Anna Weyel's "register of births", 1884-1917
(identifies country of birth of parents); Oliver-Jayne Family
Papers (Scottish origins, memoirs); Stevens Family Papers;
James Alexander Papers; account books of Thomas Nesbitt, 1787
-1825, & John Mehelm, 1733-1774;   Record Book of Great King
Hole Mine, 1838-1849.
Published finding aids: Shemer & Morris, Guide to the MS
Collections of the New Jersey Historical Society (NJHS, 1979).

174. NEWARK MUSEUM
              43-49 Washington Street
              Newark, N.J.   07101
              (201) 733-6600
       Hours: 12-5 M-Sat.
              1-5 Sun.
       Access: Advance written request required.
       NO copying facilities.
Sources:
Hamer, NHPRC (Materials, from 1619, include indentures,
business records, & papers of New Jersey families).
Published finding aids: None.

175. RED BANK PUBLIC LIBRARY
              84 West Front Street
              Red Bank, N.J.   07701
              (201) 842-0690
       Hours: 9-8 M,W,Th.
              9-5 T,F, Sat.
       Access: Open for reference to non-residents.
       Copying facilities.
Sources:
New Jersey Room Collection (genealogical, biographical, &
historical materials); newspapers, periodicals (include Red
Bank Register, 1878-present); vertical file (city/county
history, biography, genealogy); General Collection (addition-
al materials).
Published finding aids: None.

176. FAIRLEIGH DICKINSON UNIVERSITY
              Messler Library, New Jersey Room
              Rutherford, N.J.   07070
              (201) 933-5000
       Hours: 9-10 M-W.
              8:30-4:30 Th-F.
       Access: Query first.
       Copying facilities.
Sources:

NHPRC (Materials, from 1694, relate to state and local history of N.J.; political papers of Fairleigh S. Dickinson, Jr., Rutherford-Russell-Watts Family Collection; Farrett A. Hobart Papers; John S. Schultze Papers; land surveys, day books, receipts from medicine, law, trade, & agriculture).
Published finding aids: None.

177.   NEW JERSEY DIVISION OF ARCHIVES & RECORDS MANAGEMENT
       New Jersey Dept. of State
       CN 307, 185 West Street
       Trenton, N.J.   08625
       (609) 292-6260 or 6265
       Hours: 8:30-4:30 M-F.
              9-5 Sat.
       Access: Open.
       Copying facilities.
Sources:
Wills, deeds, marriage bonds, court records (including naturalization), military records, passenger lists, county records; State Legislation records; Morris Canal records; railroad files; Dept. of State records (Part of New Jersey State Library until 1983).
Published finding aids: "Genealogical Research: A Guide to Source Materials in the Archives & History Bureau of N.J. State Library" (1971).

178.   NEW JERSEY STATE LIBRARY
       CN 520 185 W. State Street
       Trenton, N.J.   08625
       (609) 292-6260
       Hours: 8:30-4:30 M-F.
              9-5 Sat.
       Access: Open.
       Copying facilities.
Sources:
New Jersey state and family history from 1663; collection includes vital records, Federal censuses, newspapers, county records, deedes, tax records, marriage records, and Naturalization records. (See also #177, N.J. Div. of Archives).
Published finding aids: "Genealogical Research: A Guide to Source Materials in the Archives & History Bureau of N.J. State Library" (1971).

NEW MEXICO

179.   UNIVERSITY OF NEW MEXICO
       Zimmerman Library, Special Collections
       Albuquerque, N.M.   87131
       (505) 277-6451
       Hours: 8-4:30 M-F.
       Access: Open.
       Copying facilities.

Sources:
NHPRC (Materials, from 1462, focus on New Mexico & the Southwest, but include other areas of U.S., Mexico, Spain, France,
and England; land-grants, maps, private papers, business
records).
Published finding aids: None.

180. HIGH PLAINS HISTORICAL FOUNDATION, INC.
        313 Prairieview & Clovis-Carter Public Library
        115 West Eighth/ Rt. 2, Box 152
        Clovis, N.M. 88101
        (505) 985-2479, or 762-9535
      Hours: By appointment.
      Access: By permission.
      Copying facilities.
Sources:
NHPRC (Materials, from 1883, include personal histories of
pioneers, scrapbooks, cassette interviews, cemetery lists,
correspondence).
Published finding aids: None.

181. NEW MEXICO STATE UNIVERSITY LIBRARY
        Rio Grande Historical Collection
        Las Cruces, N.M. 88003
        (505) 646-3731
      Hours: 8-5 M-F.
      Access: Open.
      Copying facilities.
Sources:
NHPRC (Materials, from 1850, include N.M. documentary mater-
ials, such as records of individuals & families, records of
organizations, business records, & records of social clubs).
Published finding aids: None.

182. NEW MEXICO STATE RECORDS CENTER & ARCHIVES
        404 Montezuma
        Santa Fe, N.M. 87503
        (505) 827-8860
      Hours: 8-5 M-F.
      Access: Open.
      Copying facilities.
Sources:
Materials, from 1621, include records, private papers, & col-
lections relating to New Mexico history; Spanish & Mexican
Archives, 1621-1846 (include government/State/church/military
records); personal & business papers from Spanish period to
present; naturalization records, 1870-1900.
Published finding aids: None.

183. SILVER CITY MUSEUM
        312 West Broadway
        Silver City, N.M. 88061
        (505) 538-5921
      Hours: 9-4:30 T-F.
             9-1   Sat.
             1-4   Sun.

       Access: Open.
       Copying facilities.
Sources:
NHPRC (Materials, from 1870, include Silver City & Grant Co.
records - mortuary, hardware store, sheriff's record book,
mining documents, hotel register, & tax rolls.
Published finding aids: None.

NEW YORK

184. NEW YORK STATE ARCHIVES
       New York State Dept. of Education
       Cultural Education Center, Empire State Plaza
       Albany, N.Y. 12230
       (518) 474-1195
       Hours: 8:30-5 M-F.
       Access: Open.
       Copying facilities.
Sources:
NHPRC (Materials, from 1640, include a large collection of
N.Y. colonial records, land records, council minutes, since
the Revolution; also, prison records, state censuses, papers
of Governors, and other executive records).
Published finding aids: None.

185. BROOKLYN PUBLIC LIBRARY
       History Division
       Grand Army Plaza
       Brooklyn, N.Y. 11238
       (718) 780-7794
       Hours: 9-8 M-Th.
             10-6 F-Sat.
       Access: Open, but appointment advisable.
       Copying facilities.
Sources:
Brooklyn local history, books, maps, extensive clipping file,
photos, manuscripts; Kings County town records, Brooklyn daily
newspapers on microfilm. NOT genealogically oriented.
Published finding aids: None.

186. LONG ISLAND HISTORICAL SOCIETY
       128 Pierrepont Street
       Brooklyn, N.Y. 11201
       (718) 624-0890
       Hours: 9-5 T-Sat.
       Access: Fee for non-members.
       Copying facilities.
Sources:
Collection, from 1650, covers the history of Brooklyn & Long
Island, including papers & journals, deeds, ms, maps, genealo-
gical ms, & records of organizations, businesses, & churches.
Published finding aids: Accession notes in _Journal of Long_

Island History, 1961-69, & 1973 - on.

187. ST. FRANCIS COLLEGE
            James A. Kelly Local Historical Studies Inst.
            180 Remsen Street
            Brooklyn, N.Y.   11201
            (718) 522-2300
      Hours: 9-5 M-F.
      Access: Open to the public.
      No copying facilities.
Sources:
Materials, from 1643, include records of the six original
towns of Kings County (i.e., Gravesend, Flatbush, New Utrecht,
Flatlands, Bushwick, & Brooklyn) through 1898; special col-
lections include Cong. John Rooney Papers, Minutes of Friendly
Sons of St. Patrick, John C. Malone materials, documents of
Brooklyn Common Council, Kings County Supervisors Minutes,
and Irish American sheet music.
Published finding aids: None.

188. EAST HAMPTON FREE LIBRARY
            Long Island Collection
            159 Main Street
            East Hampton, N.Y.   11937
            (516) 324-0221
      Hours: 1-4:30 T-Th. & Sat.
      Access: Open.
      Copying facilities.
Sources:
From 17th century to present - letters, journals, logbooks,
account books, & other records, biographical materials; The
Seversmith Collection; Jeannette Edwards Rattray Collection;
local histories, family histories, census returns, & more.
Published finding aids: None.

189. CRANDALL LIBRARY
            City Park
            Glens Falls, N.Y.   12801
            (518) 792-6508
      Hours: 9-9 M-Th.
             9-5 F & Sat.
      Access: Open.
      Copying facilities.
Sources:
Materials, from 1860, relate to the history & development of
the state, especially the northeastern section, with emphasis
on the history of Warren, Washington, Saratoga, & Hamilton
counties, and the towns of Glens Falls, Queensbury, Moreau,
and adjacent communities. Major collections: Holder & Miller.
Census records, directories, family genealogies.
Published finding aids: Guide to Historical Resources in
Warren County, N.Y. (Cornell, c. 1982); Guide to Local
Historical Materials (Saratoga Springs, 1977).

190.   CORNELL UNIVERSITY DEPT. OF MANUSCRIPTS & ARCHIVES
           101 John M. Olin Library
           Ithaca, N.Y. 14853
           (607) 256-3530
       Hours: 8-5 M-F.
              9-1 Sat.
       Access: Open to qualified researchers.
       Copying facilities.
Sources:
George Hyde Clarke Family Papers, 1705-1937, 1965 (business,
land and family papers of eight generations); Devereux Family
Papers, 1800-1942; Moore Family Papers, 1751-1939 (includes
Londonderry marriage contract & will); Hannah Gould Johnson
Stoddard Collection, 1878-1965; Harriet Berry Tyson Collec-
tion; J.F. Wilde correspondence; genealogical materials -
Allen - Young; Ball-Lee Business Records, 1821-1881; Bond
& Grayston Immigrant Letters, 1870-1899; Hails/Dawson Letters;
Kernan Family Papers, 1766-1922; David Laing Immigrant Letters
1873-76; Scottish Immigrant Accounts, 1825-53; John Wilson
Immigrant Letters, 1849; McNish Family Papers, 1773-1853;
Stevenson Family Papers; Ezra Cornell Letters; and many more.
Published finding aids: Reports of the Curator, 1942-45, 1945
-46, 1946-48, 1948-50; Reports of the Curator and Archivist,
1950-54, 1954-58, 1958-62, 1962-66. Also Documentation News-
letter, twice yearly, Spring 1975 - present.

191.   QUEENS BOROUGH PUBLIC LIBRARY
           Long Island Division
           89-11 Merrick Blvd.
           Jamaica, N.Y. 11432
           (718) 990-0770
       Hours: 10-9 M & F.
              10-6 T., W., Th.
              10-5:30 Sat.
       Access: Open to adults.
       Copying facilities.
Sources:
Materials refer to the Long Island area (i.e., counties of
Kings, Queens, Nassau, & Suffolk) and include Arthur D. Benson "Genealogical Notes Concerning The Benson Family", William
A. Eardeley "Genealogical Notes", Herbert F. Seversmith "Genealogical Work Papers", and smaller collections of personal
papers; vertical file on 450-500 families, card file listing
specific sources of data on certain individuals.
Published finding aids: None, but typescript aids exist for
all collections.

192.   AMERICAN IRISH HISTORICAL SOCIETY
           991 Fifth Avenue
           New York, N.Y. 10028
           (212) 288-2263
       Hours: 12-7 T-F.
              10-5 Sat.
       Access: Open.
       No copying facilities.
Sources:

Papers of Daniel F. Cohalan, Donal O'Callahan, Thomas O'Connor & others; records of Friends of Irish Freedom, Society of Friendly Sons of St. Patrick, American Irish Historical Society, Ancient Order of Hibernians, Guild of Catholic Lawyers, Catholic Club of New York, etc.; pictorial collection.
Published finding aids: None.

193. COLUMBIA UNIVERSITY LIBRARY
            801 Butler Library
            New York, N.Y. 10027
            (212) 280-2231, or -2232
      Hours: 9-5 M-F.
      Access: Open to qualified scholars.
      Copying facilities.
Sources:
Collections relate to Irish in politics - Edward P. Kilroe Papers (36 vols., 17 boxes), and Tammany Society Papers, 1776 -1952.
Published finding aids: Columbia Library Columns, pub. 3 times per year.

194. MUNICIPAL ARCHIVES & RECORDS CENTER
            31 Chambers Street
            New York, N.Y. 10007
            (212) 566-5292
      Hours: 9:30-4:30 M-F.
      Access: Open, but fee for use.
      Copying facilities.
Sources:
Official birth records - Manhattan, 1847-97, Brooklyn, 1866-97; marriages - Manhattan, 1847-65.
Published finding aids: None.

195. NEW YORK CITY DEPARTMENT OF HEALTH
            Bureau of Vital Records
            125 Worth Street
            New York, N.Y. 10013
            (212) 619-4530 & 285-9503
      Hours: 8:30-4:30 M-F.
      Access: Fee per record.
      Copying facilities.
Sources:
Official birth & death records, since 1897, all boroughs. (Earlier ones at Municipal Archives & Records; and marriage records are at offices of City Clerks in the 5 boroughs).
Published finding aids: None.

196. NEW YORK GENEALOGICAL & BIOGRAPHICAL SOCIETY
            122 East 58th Street
            New York, N.Y. 10022
            (212) 755-8532
      Hours: 9:30-5 M-Sat.
      Access: Fee charged; non-circulating materials.
      Copying facilities.
Sources:
NHPRC, Hamer, NUCMC, 1976 (Holdings include genealogical,

biographical, & historical materials from Colonial times to
present, expecially church records & cemetery inscriptions).
Published finding aids: NY G. & B. Record (1870 to date).

197.   NEW YORK HISTORICAL SOCIETY
            170 Central Park West
            New York, N.Y.   10024
            (212) 873-4300
            Hours: 10-5   T-Sat.
            Access: Non-members need permission.
            Copying facilities.
Sources:
Alexander Papers, Livingston Papers, Bohman Papers, Banyar
Papers, Alexander Knox Papers, Irish Immigrant Papers, Eng-
lish Immigrant Papers, Scots Immigrant Papers, diaries,
letters, reminiscences; extensive holdings of business re-
cords, miscellaneous records, including records relating to
Canada, 1694-1814.
Published finding aids: Breton's Guide to the MS Collections
of NYHS (Greenwood Press, 1972).

198.   NEW YORK PUBLIC LIBRARY
            Manuscript & Archives Division
            5th Avenue & 42nd Street
            New York, N.Y.   10018
            (212) 790-6338
            Hours: 1-6   M-W, F & Sat.
            Access: Qualified researchers only.
            Copying facilities.
Sources:
Documents relating to the American Revolution (diaries,
logbooks, account books); U.S. Presidential Papers; personal
& organizational papers; large collections include John
Jacob Astor Papers, 1792-1843; Andrew Carnegie Papers, 1890
-1946; Samuel Gompers Papers, George Bancroft Collection,
1585-1883; the Thomas A. Emmett Collection; the DeCoursey
Fales Collection; Wm. J.A. Maloney Irish Historical Collection; and the American Loyalist Transcripts.
Published finding aids: Dictionary Catalog of the MS Division (G.K. Hall, 1967, 2 vols.); Sam P. Williams Guide to
the Research Collections of NYPL (Ala., 1975).

199.   SUFFOLK COUNTY HISTORICAL SOCIETY
            300 West Main Street
            Riverhead, N.Y.   11901
            (516) 727- 2881
            Hours: 12:30-4:30   M-Sat.
            Access: No loans.
            Copying facilities.
Sources:
Materials, from 1640, include data on immigrants to Suffolk
County, primarily from England. Collection not indexed.
Published finding aids: None.

200. ROCHESTER PUBLIC LIBRARY
          Local History Division
          115 South Avenue
          Rochester, N.Y.   14604
          (716) 428-7338
      Hours: 9-9   M-Th.
             9-6   F.
             10-4 Sat. (Oct. - May only).
      Access: Open.
      Copying facilities.
Sources:
City of Rochester misc. records, naturalization records
(index in city clerk's office, 30 Church Street) 1895-
1906; Jean Vance Clark Papers; St. Mary's Hospital Records,
1861-1880 (in St. Mary's Hospital, 84 Genesee Street);
Episcopal Church records; newspaper index, 1818-1903; county
histories for Genesee Valley; newspaper clipping file, 1936-
date.
Published finding aids: None.

201. CENTER FOR MIGRATION STUDIES
          Brooklyn Archives
          209 Flagg Place
          Staten Island, N.Y. 10304
          (718) 351-8800
      Hours: 9-5   M-F.
      Access: Open.
      Copying facilities.
Sources:
NHPRC (Materials, from 1880, document the immigrant experience, primarily that of Italian-Americans, and the role
of the Catholic Church in that process. Records include organizational and personal papers. Possible Irish immigrant
material).
Published finding aids: Olha della Cava, A Guide To The
Archives (1974).

202. STATEN ISLAND HISTORICAL SOCIETY
          441 Clarke Avenue
          Staten Island, N.Y.   10306
          (718) 351-1611
      Hours: 10-5   T-Sat.
             2-5   Sun.
      Access: Appointment required; user fee.
      Copying facilties.
Sources:
Materials, from 1640, include personal, family, governmental
papers, business records, church records, microfilm of dia-
ries of Hessian soldiers in America during the American
Revolution.
Published finding aids: Staten Island Historian (quarterly).

203.   ONONDAGA COUNTY PUBLIC LIBRARY
           Local History & Genealogical Dept.
           335 Montgomery Street
           Syracuse, N.Y.   13202
           (315) 473-6801
       Hours: 8:30-4:30   M-Sat.
       Access: Open.
       Copying facilities.
Sources:
Materials, from 19th century on, relating to Syracuse &
Onondaga Co., include church, cemetery, Bible, family, and
cnesus records; genealogical data about local and other
families; file card list of residents before 1850.
Published finding aids: None.

204.   UTICA PUBLIC LIBRARY
           303 Genesee Street
           Utica, N.Y.   13501
           (315) 735-2279
       Hours: 9-9   M, W, Th.
              9-5:30 T, F.
              9-5   Sat. (Sept. - June).
       Access: Open.
       Copying facilities.
Sources:
Welsh language newspaper, Y Drych (1903-1916), and other
Welsh materials; census records, cemetery records & church
records, city directories, Utica newspapers from 1825, local
histories, usual published genealogical aids.
Published finding aids: List of Family Histories in Utica
Public Library (n.d.).

205.   WESTCHESTER COUNTY HISTORICAL SOCIETY
           75 Grasslands Road
           Valhalla, N.Y.   10595
           (914) 592-4338
       Hours: 10-5   T-F.
       Access: On-site use only.
       Copying facilities.
Sources:
Materials relating to the history and genealogy of Westchester
Co.; County Alms House Record Books (23 vols, 1854-1908),
identify age, previous residence, nationality, and, in some
instances, parental data.
Published finding aids: None.

NORTH CAROLINA

206. UNIVERSITY OF NORTH CAROLINA AT CHAPEL HILL LIBRARY
          Manuscripts Dept. & Southern Historical Coll.
          Chapel Hill, N.C. 27514
          (919) 933-1345
     Hours: 8-5 M-F.
     Access: Permission necessary.
     Copying facilities.
Sources:
Materials, from 1750, include colonial documents, photostats
of selected materials from Public Records Office in London,
& much material relating to the American Revolution and early
national period; private papers of public figures from several
southern states; Anti-Bellum materials; also correspondence,
business papers, church records, diaries, account books; Reconstruction collection, late 19th century collection, 20th
century collection.
Published finding aids: The Southern Historical Collection:
A Guide to MS (CH, 1970), and the Southern Historical Collection: A Supplementary Guide.... (CH. 1975).

207. PUBLIC LIBRARY OF CHARLOTTE & MECKLENBURG COUNTY
          310 North Tryon Street
          Charlotte, N.C. 28202
          (704) 374-2725
     Hours: 9-9 M-F.
            9-5 Sat.
     Access: Open.
     Copying facilities.
Sources:
Depository for Mecklenburg Historical & Genealogical Association records; local history, family history, state and federal
census records (with Codex indexes), newspapers, card file
of family names, strong Scotch-Irish Collection.
Published finding aids: None.

208. DUKE UNIVERSITY
          William R. Perkins Library, MS Sept.
          Durham, N.C. 27706
          (919) 684-3372
     Hours: 8-5:30 M-F.
            9-12:30 Sat.
     Access: With permission.
     Copying facilities.
Sources:
Materials, from 1750, relate to the Southern States, the
Anti-Bellum South, Civil War & Reconstruction, religion,
public affairs of 19th & 20th centuries, oral collections,
Duke family.
Published finding aids: M. Russell, "MS Dept. in Duke Univer-
sity Library", American Archivist 28 (July 1965).

209 . GUILFORD COLLEGE LIBRARY
           Quaker Collection
           Greensboro, N.C.   27410
           (919) 292-5511
       Hours: 10-4 M-F.
       Access: User fee.
       Copying facilities.
Sources:
Materials, from 1680, include Records of The Society of
Friends in N.C., New Garden Boarding School, & Guilford
College; private papers of N.C. Quakers, oral histories of
Quaker national leaders & local residents; records of births,
marriages, deaths, and other data.
Published finding aids: J.F. Moore Sources of Quaker History
in N.C. (Guilford College, 1967).

210 . EAST CAROLINA UNIVERSITY
           J.Y. Joyner Library, MS Collection
           Greenville, N.C.   27834
           (919) 757-6671
       Hours: 8-5 M-F.
       Access: Open.
       Copying facilities.
Sources:
Materials, from 1750, relating to state history, military
history, missionaries, and agriculture; oral history tapes.
Published finding aids: East Carolina MS Collection Bulletin
(1969 -   ).

211. HISTORICAL FOUNDATION OF PRESBYTERIAN & REFORMED
      CHURCHES
           Georgia Terrace/ P.O. Box 847
           Montreat, N.C.   28757
           (704) 669-7061
       Hours: 8:30-4:30/5:30 M-F.
       Access: By permission.
       Copying facilities.
Sources:
Materials, from 1638, focus upon Presbyterian & Reformed
Churches of the world, the U.S.A., the South; include records
of synods & presbyteries of Presbyterian, Associate Presbyterian, and Cumberland Presbyterian Churches of South Atlantic, Southern, and other states; records of Presbyterian
organizations in other nations, papers pertaining to organization of Presbyterian Church in the U.S. in 1861, and to
subsequent reorganizations, private papers.
Published finding aids: T.H. Spence The Historical Foundation
& Its Treasures (1960).

212 . NORTH CAROLINA STATE ARCHIVES
           109 E. Jones Street
           Raleigh, N.C.   27611
           (919) 733-3952
       Hours: 8-5:30 T-F.
              8-5   Sat.
       Access: With identification.

        Copying facilities.
Sources:
Herbert Hutchinson Brimley Papers, 1861; Colin Shaw Papers,
1735-1883; C.B. Heller Collection, 1735-1923; Besson & Line-
ham Family Papers, 1774-1967; James Trotter Papers, 1824;
Margaret McIver Buie Gaelic Psalm Book (n.d.); and other
smaller personal collections; official records of colony and
state of North Carolina; papers of the governors, secretary
of state (land grants & surveys), and judiciary; military
records, wills, estate inventories, marriage bonds, tax lists,
school reports.
Published finding aids: Cain, McGrew & Morris Guide to Private
MS Collections in N.C. State Archives (1981).

213. ROWAN COUNTY PUBLIC LIBRARY
            201 West Fisher Street/ P.O. Box 4039
            Salisbury, N.C. 28144
            (704) 633-5578
        Hours: 9-5:30 M-Sat.
        Access: Open.
        Copying facilities.
Sources:
Materials, from 1720, include McCuffines & Smith Collection
of court records, deeds, wills, Bible records, genealogical
charts, & correspondence for Rowan County and "Old Irish
Town".
Published finding aids: R.B. Downes Resources of N.C. Lib-
raries (1965).

214. CLEVELAND COUNTY MEMORIAL LIBRARY
            104 Howie Drive
            Shelby, N.C. 28150
            (704) 487-9069
        Hours: 9-9 M-Th.
               9-5 F-Sat.
        Access: Open.
        Copying facilities.
Sources:
Historical & genealogical materials about Cleveland Co.,
similar data for Rutherford & Lincoln Counties prior to 1840;
95% complete court records for Cleveland Co.; family histories,
censuses, Colonial Records of North Carolina.
Published finding aids: Computer printout.

215. MORAVIAN ARCHIVES
            Drawer M, Salem Station
            Winston Salem, NC 27108
Source: Questionnaire not returned. Hamer (Materials from 1753
include some 10,000 manuscript pages relating to the settlement
of Wachovia, also church registers, account books, diaries,
minute books, memoirs, and letters).

216. WAKE FOREST UNIVERSITY
            North Carolina Baptist Historical Collection
            P.O. Box 7777, Reynolda Station
            Winston-Salem, N.C. 27109

(919) 725-9711
Hours: 8:30-4:30 M-F.
Access: Permission needed.

Copying facilities.
Sources:
Materials, from 1770, include N.C. Baptist Association &
Church Records (Southern, Primitive, & Black Baptists),
papers of Baptist leaders & university alumni.
Published finding aids: Preliminary Inventory of Church
Records in the Ethel T. Crittendon Collection (1972),
Supplement (1973).

NORTH DAKOTA

(Mostly Scandinavian settlers; few materials for topics of
this book).

217. STATE HISTORICAL SOCIETY OF NORTH DAKOTA
          Liberty Memorial Building
          Bismarck, N.D.   58505
          (701) 224-2668
Sources:
See Hamer, NUCMC 1965 (Houses State Archives; Materials relate to Territory & State; governor's papers, land company
papers, WPA Historical Records Survey, and others).

218. UNIVERSITY OF NORTH DAKOTA
          Chester Fritz Library MS Collection
          Grand Forks, N.D.   58201
          (701) 777-2617
      Hours: 8-5 M,T,Th, & F.
             8-11 W.
             7-11 Sun.
      Access: Open.
      Copying facilities.
Sources:
Materials, from 1880, include reports of governors, congress-
men & senators, Farmer's Union, Nonpartisan League, and N.D.
businesses.
Published finding aids: J.B. Davenport, Guide to the Orrin
G. Libby MS Collection... (1975).

219. STEELE COUNTY HISTORICAL SOCIETY LIBRARY
          Steele Avenue
          Hoke, N.D.   58046
          (701) 945-2394, 2444
      Hours: 2-5 Sun; others by appointment.
      Access: Permission needed.
      NO copying facilities.
Sources:
Materials, from 1882, include diaries, reminiscences & other
individual papers; records of schools, clubs, businesses &
government.
Published finding aids: None.

OHIO

220. UNIVERSITY OF AKRON
            Bierce Library
            Archival Services
            Akron, OH. 44325
            (216) 375-7670
        Hours: 8-5 M-F.
        Access: Adult usage.
        Copying facilities.
Sources:
Materials, from 1827, include government, business, personal,
and organizational papers and records for the eight county
area this American History Research Center serves. Materials
on the rubber industry, & lighter-than-air flight.
Published finding aids: None.

221. OHIO UNIVERSITY LIBRARY
            Special Collections
            Athens, OH. 45701
            (614) 594-5756
        Hours: 8-5 M-F.
        Access: Open.
        Copying facilities.
Sources:
Materials, from 1790's, include The University Archives,
ms collections relating to Southeastern Ohio, and local
government records.
Published finding aids: None.

222. BOWLING GREEN STATE UNIVERSITY
            Northwest Ohio-Great Lakes Research Center
            5th Floor, University Library
            Bowling Green, OH. 43403
            (419) 372-2411
        Hours: 8:30-4:30 M-F.
        Access: Open.
        Copying facilities.
Sources:
Materials, from 1814, include history of 19 northwestern Ohio
counties, records of county and city governments, churches,
businesses, railroads, and charitable organizations; extensive Great Lakes Collection, including shipslogs, diaries, &
correspondence.
Published finding aids: D.R. Larson, Guide to MS Collections
and Institutional Records in Ohio (SOA, 1974).

223. STARK COUNTY DISTRICT LIBRARY
            Reference Dept., Genealogy Collection
            715 Market Avenue North
            Canton, OH. 44702-1080
            (216) 452-0665
        Hours: 9-9 M-Th.
               9-5 F-Sat.
        Access: Open.

Copying facilities.
Sources:
U.S. Census Records - Ohio, 1820-1880, Pennsylvania - 1800,
1810, 1820; census indexes for other states; Stark County
Courthouse Records (birth, death, marriage, wills, inventor-
ies, guardianship, naturalization records), cemetery index
(card file), list of family associations & their leaders.
Published finding aids: Genealogy Collection (SCDL, 1982).

224. CINCINNATI HISTORICAL SOCIETY
        Eden Park
        Cincinnati, OH. 45202
        (513) 241-4622
      Hours: 9-4:30 T-Sat.
      Access: Open.
      Copying facilities.
Sources:
Gilligan Funeral Home Records, 1877-1961; Caledonian Society
Minute Book, 1827-1915; numerous church records, diaries, &
local histories.
Published finding aids: None.

225. UNIVERSITY OF CINCINNATI
        Archives & Rare Books Dept.
        M.L. #113
        Cincinnati, OH. 45221
        (513) 475-6459
      Hours: 12-5 M & F
             8-5 T - Th.
      Access: Permission necessary.
      Copying facilities.
Sources:
Materials, from 1830, include governmental, business, personal, & organizational papers & records for the 8 county
Southwestern Ohio area the Center serves; Hamilton County
declarations of intent, 1840-90; Hamilton Co. naturalizations,
1840-90; Brown Co. naturalizations, 1833-34.
Published finding aids: Inventories To County Records; Archives Booklet.

226. WESTERN RESERVE HISTORICAL SOCIETY
        10825 East Boulevard
        Cleveland, OH. 44106
        (216) 721-5722
      Hours: 9-5 T-Sat.
      Access: Fee for non-members.
      Copying facilities.
Sources:
Censuses for U.S., 1790-1900, 1910 Census for Ohio; complete
1880 Soundex for all states, 1900 Soundex for 6 states; 1890
Special Census of Union Veterans & Widows, Ohio only; passen-
ger lists for N.Y. & Baltimore; St. Andrews Scottish Benevo-
lent Society Records, 1848-1962; Wm. Manning (Irish) Diaries,
1863-1878; various Ohio Welsh Synod Records, 1864-1934.
Published finding aids: A Guide to the MS & Archives of the
Western Reserve Historical Society (WRHS, 1972).

227. OHIO HISTORICAL SOCIETY
           1985 Velma Avenue
           Columbus, OH.   43211
           (614) 466-1500
      Hours: 9-5 T-Sat.
      Access: Fee for non-members.
      Copying facilities.
Sources:
Materials, from 1731, include John Patterson McLean Papers,
1887-1926; Welsh Hills Families, 1801-1974 (Price, Jones,
Powell, etc.); Thomas Bissell's letters to Monoghan, 1840;
Index to Franklin Co. Naturalization Records, 1850-1906; many
naturalization records, Franklin Co. Declaration of Intent
Records, 1856-1906.
Published finding aids: MS Catalogue; Archives Catalog; Books
Catalogs.

228. WRIGHT STATE UNIVERSITY LIBRARY
           Dept. of Archives & Special Collections
           Dayton, OH. 45435
           (513) 873-2092
      Hours: 8:30-5 M-F.
      Access: On-premise use only.
      Copying facilities.
Sources:
Local government records for 12 Ohio counties; correspondence,
scrapbooks, diaries, & other papers of individuals; naturalization records (include Declaration of Intent and Final Papers)
from early 19th c. until 1906 for 11 counties. Most records
are indexed.
Published finding aids: Guide to Local Government Records
at Wright State University (n.d.).

229. KENT STATE UNIVERSITY LIBRARIES
           American History Research Center
           Kent, OH. 44242
           (216) 672-2411
      Hours: 8-5 M-F.
      Access: Open.
      Copying facilities.
Sources:
Materials, from 1792, relate to the 8 northeastern county
area served by the Center; include records of International
Brotherhood of Pottery & Allied Workers, papers of Rep.
Charles A. Mosher, county governments, and the Diocese of
Youngstown.
Published finding aids: None.

230. MARYSVILLE PUBLIC LIBRARY
           231 S. Court Street
           Marysville, OH. 43040
           (513) 644-9290
      Hours: 10-8 M,T, & Th.
             10-5 W,F, & Sat.
      Access: Open.
      Copying facilities.

Sources:
Cemetery records, family collections (Adams, Ball, Blue,
Cooper, Jarboe, Trumbo, and others), local histories, wills,
marriage & birth records, newspapers on microfilm.
Published finding aids: None.

231. TOLEDO - LUCAS COUNTY PUBLIC LIBRARY
            Local History Dept.
            325 Michigan Street
            Toledo, OH. 43624
            (419) 255-7055
        Hours: 9-9 M-Th.
               9-5:30 F-Sat.
        Access: On-site use only.
        Copying facilities.
Sources:
Materials, from 1800, include pioneer history & local history,
The War of 1812, Civil War, & late 19th - early 20th centur-
ies, photographs, 19th c. maps.
Published finding aids: None.

232. MUSKINGUM COUNTY GENEALOGICAL LIBRARY
            1425 Newark Road
            Zanesville, OH. 43701
            (614) 452-0729
        Hours: 8-9 M-F.
        Access: Reference only; adults only.
        Copying facilities.
Sources:
Family histories, memoirs, census on microfilm, Ohio Land
Grant records, tax records, Muskingum newspapers, obits,
many published genealogical tools.
Published finding aids: None.

OKLAHOMA

233. MUSEUM OF THE GREAT PLAINS
            Library & Archives
            601 Ferris/ P.O. Box 68
            Lawton, OK. 73501
            (405) 353-5675
        Hours: 8-5 M-F.
        Access: Open.
        Copying facilities.
Sources:
WPA Records, political papers of Fred Harris, T.P. Gore,
Scott Ferris, & L.M. Gensman.
Published finding aids: None.

234. UNIVERSITY OF OKLAHOMA LIBRARY
              Western History Collection
              Division of MS
              630 Parrington Oval
              Norman, OK. 73019
              (405) 325-3641
              Hours: 8-5 M-F.
              Access: Open.
              Copying facilities.
Sources:
Settlers diaries, journals, & correspondence, business papers,
papers of Oklahoma governors and congressional members, pa-
pers of economic leaders, materials relating to the American
West and Southwest.
Published finding aids: A.M. Gibson Guide to Regional MS
Collections ...U. of Oklahoma Library (1960).

235. OKLAHOMA ARCHIVES & RECORDS DIVISION
              Oklahoma Dept. of Libraries
              200 Northeast 18th Street
              Oklahoma City, OK. 73105
              (405) 521-2502
              Hours: 8-5 M-F.
              Access: Open.
              Copying facilities.
Sources:
Materials, from 1890, include government records (legislative,
judicial, executive) since 1907, and some territorial records,
1890-1907; records of U.S. Land Offices; records of Oklahoma
Historical Records Survey.
Published finding aids: None.

236. OKLAHOMA HERITAGE ASSOCIATION ARCHIVES
              201 Northwest 14th Street
              Oklahoma City, OK. 73103
              (405) 235-4458
              Hours: 9-4 M-F.
              Access: By appointment.
              Copying facilities.
Sources:
Materials, from 1889, focus on 400+ prominent Oklahomans;
newspaper clippings, & other materials on state & local
history.
Published finding aids: None.

OREGON

237. SOUTHERN OREGON HISTORICAL SOCIETY
              Jacksonville Museum, Archives & Library
              206 N. 5th Street
              Jacksonville, OR. 97530
              (503) 899-1847

Hours: 9-5 M-Sat.
Access: Permission needed.
Copying facilities.
Sources:
Materials, from 1845, focus on Southwestern Oregon, especially
Jackson County, 1850-1920; includes letters, diaries, Jackson
Co. Archives, archives of city of Jacksonville, & those of
business firms & organizations.
Published finding aids: None.

238. ARCHDIOCESE OF PORTLAND IN OREGON
        History & Archives Dept.
        2838 East Burnside
        Portland, OR. 97207
        (503) 234-5334
        Hours: 8:15-4:45 M-F.
        Access: Permission.
        NO copying facilities.
Sources:
Materials, from 1840, cover Roman Catholic Church history
in Oregon & Pacific Northwest, includes genealogical data
from parishes, churches, & archives, diocesian correspondence, account books, and other business records.
Published finding aids: None.

239. GENEALOGICAL FORUM OF PORTLAND, OREGON, INC.
        1410 S.W. Morrison Street, Suite 812
        Portland, OR. 97205
        (503) 227-2398
        Hours: 9:30-3 M-W, F & Sat.
               9:30-8:30   Th.
        Access: Open, but fees after first visit.
        Copying facilities.
Sources:
Family histories, material in vertical file.
Published finding aids: Library Shelf List of the Genealogi-
cal Forum of Portland (GFP, 1983).

240. OREGON HISTORICAL SOCIETY
        1230 S.W. Park Avenue
        Portland, OR. 97205
        (503) 222-1741
        Hours: 10-4:45 M-Sat.
        Access: Open.
        Copying facilities.
Sources:
British Residents of Oregon, Papers, 1886-1970 (minutes,
correspondence, financial records, legal documents); Pioneer
Register, 1805-59 (names, birthplaces, & some biographical
data); Ethnology - miscellaneous, ca. 1850's-1970's; per-
sonal papers; some microfilm from British Museum, Public
Records Office in London, and elsewhere.
Published finding aids: Oregon Historical Society MS Collec-
tion (Portland, 1971).

241.   OREGON STATE ARCHIVES & RECORDS CENTER
             1001 Broadway NE
             Salem, OR. 97310
             (503) 378-4240
        Hours: 805 M-F.
        Access: Open to public.
        Copying facilities.
Sources:
Materials, from 1843, include state government records &
related materials; Williamette Cattle Company records, 1837-
- ; records of 23 counties & 4 cities; WPA Records, 1935-40;
U.S. Census schedules, 1850, '60, '70, & '80; naturalization
records for some counties.
Published finding aids: None.

242.   OREGON STATE LIBRARY
             State Library Building
             Summer & Court Streets
             Salem, OR. 97310-0640
             (503) 378-4243
        Hours: 8-5 M-F.
        Access: Open.
        Copying facilities.
Sources:
Hamer (Materials include Papers of Asahel Bush & family,
1837-1938; papers of John Minto, 1864-1912; business & family
papers of the Capitol National Bank, 1885-1922, & the Capitol
Lumbering Company, 1853-1934; records of the Oregon Voter,
1917-47; repository for records, Missionary District of
Eastern Oregon of the Episcopal Church, 1870-1956).
Published finding aids: Nothing current.

PENNSYLVANIA

243.   U.S. ARMY MILITARY HISTORY INSTITUTE
             Carlisle Barracks
             Carlisle, PA. 17013-5008
             (717) 245-3611
        Hours: 8-4:30 M-F.
        Access: Some materials require security clearance.
        Copying facilities.
Sources:
(The Institute was formerly known as the U.S. Army Military
History Research Collection).
See NUCMC, 1975-76, & Hamer. (Materials, from 1600, focus on
military and U.S. history. Included are diaries, personal
letters, memoirs, copies of official letters, relating to
Militia, Volunteer, & Regular Land Forces. Materials from
other services; archives of the Army War College; strong
Civil War Collection).
Published finding aids: Manuscript Holdings of the Military
History Research Collection (1972-75).

244.   BALCH INSTITUTE FOR ETHNIC STUDIES
              185 7th Street
              Philadelphia, PA. 19106
              (215) 925-8090
        Hours: 9-5 M-Sat.
        Access: Open.
        Copying facilities.
Sources:
Sizable collection of books and pamphlets on all topics of
this directory. Notable ms collections are Curtis Family
Papers, 1845-57; Dennis Clark Papers (research files & other
papers of a historian); Ignatius Donnelly Papers, 1836-43;
Costillo Family Papers, 1827-1874; Michael Doyle's reminis-
cences of San Francisco; five Irish-American newspapers, 1849
-1951. (See also Entries # 250 & #251)
Published finding aids: New Dimensions (Quarterly newsletter)
& Selected List of Newspaper & MS Holdings (BIES, n.d.).

245.   CITY ARCHIVES OF PHILADELPHIA
              Room 523, City Hall Annex
              Philadelphia, PA. 19107
              (215) MU6-2276/ 2249
        Hours: 8:30-5 M-F.
        Access: Open, but no photos by patrons.
        Copying facilities.
Sources:
Court of Common Pleas - declarations of intention of naturalization, 1821-1911, and petitions for naturalization, 1794-
1903; Court of Quarter Sessions and Oyer & Terminer - declarations of intentions for naturalizations, 1802-1906, 1913-30,
and petitions of naturalization, 1800-1897, & 1913-1930;
District Court - declarations of intentions... 1818-75 &
petitions...1811-74; Court of General Sessions - declaration
...1839-43; Guardians of the Poor-Ship & Passenger Lists,
1859-67, and register, receipts of capital tax on ship passenger arrivals, 1839-77, & ship register, 1839-43.
Published finding aids: None.

246.   FEDERAL ARCHIVES & RECORDS CENTER
              c/o Regional Archivist
              9th & Market Sts.
              Philadelphia, PA. 19107
              (215) 597-3000
        Hours: 8-5 M-F.
              9-1 (ist & 3rd Sat.)
        Access: Most collections open.
        Copying facilities.
Sources:
(Serves DE., PA., MD., VA., & W.V.). Records of District
Courts of U.S. (Civil, Criminal, Admiralty, & Bankruptcy)
until the 1950's; Records of United Courts of Appeals, 1891-
1950's; Records of Bureau of Indian Affairs; Records of
Customs; Records of Office of the Chief of Engineers; census
records; NARC Microfilms (genealogy/ethnology).
Published finding aids: Research Opportunities (General Ser-
vices Administration: National Archives &Records Service, 1980)

247. GENEALOGICAL SOCIETY OF PENNSYLVANIA
           1300 Locust Street
           Philadelphia, PA.   19107
           (215) 545-0391
        Hours: 1-9 M.
               9-5 T-F.
        Access: Fee for non-members.
        NO copying facilities.
Sources:
Materials, from 1620, include family histories, census re-
cords, city directories, oaths of allegiance, immigration
records, church records, undertaker's records, cemetery re-
cords, wills and administrations, & orphan court records for
Pennsylvania, chiefly.
Published finding aids: PA. Genealogical Magazine.

248. HISTORICAL SOCIETY OF PENNSYLVANIA
           1300 Locust Street
           Philadelphia, PA.   19107
           (215) 732-6200
        Hours: 1-9 M.
               9-5 T.
        Access: Fee for non-members; open only to qualified,
               experienced persons.
        Copying facilities.
Sources:
Etting Collection, 1558-1917 (includes Quaker letters, 1650
-1815); Gilbert Cope Collection; James Logan Collection;
John Dickinson & Family Collection; Penn. ms., 1606-1874;
Cadawalader Family Collection, 1630-1900; Edward Carey
Gardner Collection; Gilpin Family Papers, 1727-1872; Hollings-
worth Family, 1748-1887; papers of military officers, business
leaders and businesses (numerous bank records); records of
Penn. counties; and more.
Published finding aids: Guide to the MS Collections of the
Historical Society of Pennsylvania (2nd ed., 1949).

249. PENNSYLVANIA HISTORICAL & MUSEUM COMMISSION
           Bureau of Archives & History
           Box 1026/ 3rd & Forester Streets
           Harrisburg, PA.   17120
           (717) 787-3023
        Hours: 8:30-4:45 M-F.
        Access: Open, but some materials restricted.
        Copying facilities.
Sources:
Strong collection, from 1664, includes records of all branches
of state government, genealogical & immigration materials -
passenger lists, naturalization records, vital statistics,
military & war records, records by occupation, prison records,
land records, church & cemetery records, county records,
census records, miscellaneous records, & family papers (521
c.f. Achey to Zehner-Zaner).
Published finding aids: R.M. Dructor, Guide to Genealogical
Sources at the Pennsylvania State Archives (PHMC, 1981).

250.   PRESBYTERIAN HISTORICAL SOCIETY
            425 Lombard Street
            Philadelphia, PA. 19147
            (215) 627-1852
        Hours: 9-5 M-F.
        Access: Non-circulating materials.
        Copying facilities.
Sources:
Archives of the United Presbyterian Church in the U.S.A.;
records of National Council of Churches, the American Sunday
School Union, American Foreign and Christian Union, and the
National Temperance Society. Church records include minutes
& files of General Assemblies, synods, presbyteries, & individual congregations of a dozen American & Reformed Presbyterian denominations; files include foreign & domestic
missions, women's work in the church, immigrant and ethnic
minority work; the Sheldon Jackson Collection on the American
West & Alaska; papers of John Dabney Shane, Albert Barnes,
John Wilbur Chapman, Henry Van Dyke, & Eugene Carson Blake.
Published finding aids: None, but descriptions of some collections are in Journal of Prebyterian History.(See # 244)

251.   SCOTCH-IRISH FOUNDATION
            Library & Archives
            c/o Balch Institute of Ethnic Studies
            18 S. 7th Street
            Philadelphia, PA. 19106
            (215) 925-8090
        Hours: 9-5 M-Sat.
        Access: Open.
        Copying facilities.
Sources:
(Was housed in the custody of Presbyterian Historical Society,
but moved to Balch Inst., 1985).
Library Collection includes society proceedings, newspapers,
periodicals, and bound volumes from ca. 1850; Archives in-
clude records and correspondence of the Scotch-Irish Society
of Pennsylvania and of the U.S.A., & of the Scotch-Irish
Foundation. Notable are family registrations, Adamson through
Woodburn. (See # 244)
Published finding aids: Library & Archives of the Scotch-
Irish Foundation (Phila., 1979), Supplement A (1981), &
Supplement B (1984).

252.   TEMPLE UNIVERSITY LIBRARIES
            Special Collections Department
            13th & Berks Streets
            Philadelphia, PA. 19122
            (215) 787-8230
        Hours: 9-5 M-F.
        Access: Urban Archives open; National Immigration
                Archives not open to general patrons.
        Copying facilities.
Sources:
Urban Archives Center materials, from 1850, include records
of 60 private agencies and a dozen individuals in the more

than 125 collections dealing with social services, housing,
planning, politics, education, criminal justice, & labor.
National Immigration Archives (housed in the Balch Inst. of
Ethnic Studies) include U.S. passenger manifests, East Coast,
ca. 1820-1900; a research collection transferring data (e.g.,
names and ages) of immigrants from original documents to
computer.
(See The Famine Immigrants...Irish Immigrants Arriving at
the Port of New York, 1846-1897 (Balt. Genealogy Pub. Co.).
Published finding aids: Urban Archives Notes.

253.   UNIVERSITY OF PENNSYLVANIA LIBRARIES
            Special Collections
            Van Pelt Library
            3420 Walnut Street
            Philadelphia, PA   19104
Sources: Questionnaire not returned. Hamer, NCMUC, & NHPRC
(Materials, since 1740, include some 85,000 biographical
folders, papers of political and cultural leaders, university
records, and personal papers of faculty members).

254.   UNIVERSITY OF PITTSBURGH LIBRARIES
            Pittsburgh, PA.   15260
            (412) 624-4400
        Hours: 8:30-5 M-F.
        Access: Open to scholars.
        Copying facilities.
Sources:
Materials, from 1680, focus upon the American Revolution,
include papers concerning H.H. Brackenridge, H.M. Brackenridge, Robert McKnight, and the Pitt Family; Western PA,
early history & travel; Southwestern Penn. (city & county
government agency records).
Published finding aids: None.

255.   FRIENDS HISTORICAL LIBRARY OF SWARTHMORE COLLEGE
            Swarthmore, PA.   19081
            (215) 447-7496
        Hours: 8:30-4:30 M-F.
               9-12   Sat.
        Access: Open.
        Copying facilities.
Sources:
World's largest collection of Quaker meeting archives;
monthly meetings include records of marriages, births, deaths,
and removals; microfilm copies of British Quaker records, &
microfilm copies of birth, deaths, and marriages for many
English, Irish, & Welsh meetings. Important collections of
Quaker Family papers including the Elkintons, Ferrises,
Painters, Biddles, Waltons, & Whartons.
Published finding aids: Guide to the MS Collections of Friends
Historical Library of Swarthmore College (1982).

PUERTO RICO

256. ARCHIVE GENERAL DE PUERTO RICO
          Apartado 4184
          San Juan, P.R.   00905
          (809) 722-2113
          Hours: 8-4:30 M-F.
      Access: Open.
      Copying facilities.
Sources:
Extranjeros ("Files on Foreigners"), 1807-1880 (petitions &
requirements, information on business, nationality, & resi-
dence); Preliminary Inventory of the Records of Spanish
Governors of Puerto Rico.
Published finding aids: Catalogo de extranjeros residentes
en Puerto Rico en el siglo XIX by Estela Cifre de Loubriel
(U. de PR, 1962); also inventories.

RHODE ISLAND

257. NEWPORT HISTORICAL SOCIETY
          82 Touro Street
          Newport, R.I.   02840
          (401) 846-0813
          Hours: 9:30-4:30 T-F.
                 9:30-12 noon Sat.
      Access: Fee for non-members.
      Copying facilities.
Sources:
NHPRC, NUCMC, 1966, & Hamer. (Materials, from 1650, focus on
the history of Newport & Rhode Island; include early church
records, ships logs, logbooks of prominent Newport families,
probate & custom house records, & genealogical data).
Published finding aids: None.

258. BROWN UNIVERSITY ARCHIVES
          John Carter Brown Library
          Box 1894
          Providence, R.I.   02912
          (401) 863-2725
          Hours: 8:30-5 M-F.
                 8:30-12 noon Sat.
      Access: Open to scholars.
      Copying facilities.
Sources:
Journals, ships logs, memoirs relating to R.I. history & the
colonization of America; ms maps of North & South America up
to 1830; Brown & Bartlets & Russells family histories; data
on Scots Colony of Darien.
Published finding aids: None.

259. PROVIDENCE COLLEGE ARCHIVES
            Phillips Memorial Library
            Eaton Street & River Avenue
            Providence, R.I.   02918
            (401) 865-2377
      Hours: 8:30-5:30 M-F.
      Access: Open.
      Copying facilities.
Sources:
Archives has pre-1900 court records for R.I. (FARC, Boston,
also has naturalization records for R.I.); also, includes
English & Colonial 18th Century Trade Statistics Collection
(e.g., English Customs Records, Colonial Office Records,
Summaries of Naval Office Records, Whitworth Papers and The
Gazeteer), William E. Walsh's Civil War Diary, Patrick T.
Conley Photograph Collection.
Published finding aids: An Inventory - P.T. Conley Photo-
graph Collection (P.C., 1984).

260. PROVIDENCE PUBLIC LIBRARY
            Special Collections
            150 Empire Street
            Providence, R.I.   02903
            (401) 521-7722
      Hours: By appointment.
      Access: By permission.
      Copying facilities.
Sources:
Hamer, NUCMC, 1971, NHPRC. (Materials, from 1700, include
logbooks, journals, and account books from over 1,000 whaling
voyages, & business records for the whaling industry, 1762-
1962; some 800 letters and documents, late 17th to mid-19th
century, relate to R.I. history & politics).
Published finding aids: None.

261. RHODE ISLAND HISTORICAL SOCIETY
            121 Hoke Street
            Providence, R.I.   02888
            (401) 331-8575
      Hours: 1-9 M.
             9-6 T & F.
             Hours vary in winter.
      Access: Open.
      Copying facilities.
Sources:
Materials, from 1636, are strong in records of businesses &
social organizations; important personal papers include
Moses Brown, William Ellery Channing, & Roger Williams; papers
of some Revolutionary patriots; official records of Provi-
dence, 1639-1832, and of other R.I. towns.
Published finding aids: None.

262. RHODE ISLAND STATE ARCHIVES
            Room 43, State House
            Providence, R.I.   02903
            (401) 277-2353

Hours: 8:30-4:30 M-F.
Access: Open.
Copying facilities.
Sources:
Legislative papers, state censuses, and executive & judicial
records of the Colony to date; import-export papers, ships
documents; tax lists, cities & towns, 1700-1800; probate &
land evidences (colonial); registers of R.I. vessels, 1776-
1783; military returns, papers, war records, & treasurers
accounts; maps, misc. documents.
Published finding aids: None.

SOUTH CAROLINA

263. CAMDEN ARCHIVES
            1314 Broad Street
            Camden, S.C.   29020
            (803) 432-3242
        Hours: 8-12 & 1-5 M-F.
                Sat. by appointment.
                2-5   Sun.
        Access: Sign in.
        Copying facilities.
Sources:
Trantham, Baushett, Nelson Papers, 1869-1972; Kershaw County
Medical Society Records, 1866-1951; Marriage Records of Rev.
James E. Rogers, 1852-1884; Camden City records, business
account books, district plats, 1784-1801; cemetery records
(several counties), census records, vital statistics, news-
papers, periodicals, clippings file, S.C. DAR Library, maps.
Published finding aids: None, but typed inventories are
available.
See Local and Family History in South Carolina: A Bibliography
(Charleston: S.C. Historical Society, 1981).

264. HUGUENOT SOCIETY OF SOUTH CAROLINA
            25 Chalmers Street
            Charleston, S.C.   29401
            (803) 723-3235
        Hours: 10:30-1:30 M,T,Th., & F.
        Access: Open.
        Copying facilities.
Sources:
Sizable number of pedigrees and lineage charts, minutes of
annual meetings, correspondence, books, pamphlets, newspapers.
Published finding aids: Transactions of the Huguenot Society
of South Carolina (an annual).

265. SOUTH CAROLINA HISTORICAL SOCIETY
            Fireproof Building
            Charleston, S.C.   29401
            (803) 723-3225
      Hours: 9:30-5 M-F.
             9-1   Sat.
      Access: Fee for non-members.
      Copying facilities.
Sources:
Materials, from 1520, relate to S.C., the Coastal Region, &
Charleston; include letters, diaries, travel journals, &
other papers and other important figures; records of local
governments, churches, & businesses; genealogical data,
ms maps & plats.
Published finding aids: "MS Collections of the South Carolina
Historical Society" S.C. Historical Magazine 78 (July 1977).

266. SOUTH CAROLINA DEPT. OF ARCHIVES & HISTORY
            1430 Senate Street/ P.O. Box 11669
            Columbia, S.C.   29211
            (803) 758-5816
      Hours: 9-9 M-F.
             9-6 Sat.
             1-9 Sun.
      Access: Open.
      Copying facilities.
Sources:
Materials, from 1671, include almost all known S.C. records
before 1785, nearly complete state government records to
1940, & more recent records; immigration materials are:
Grand Council Journal, 1671-92, Common House of Assembly
Journals, 1692-1775, Upper House Assembly Journals, 1721-
1768, Council Journals, 1721-74, Warrants for Land, 1672-1711,
General Assembly Papers, 1782-1868, Records of Sec. of State,
Misc. Papers, 1671-1973, County County Records (e.g., Citi-
zenry Papers); copies of papers from other repositories in-
clude Public Records Office, London, and National Archives
& Records Service.
Published finding aids: The South Carolina Archives: A
Temporary Summary Guide (S.C. D.A.H., 1976).

267. UNIVERSITY OF SOUTH CAROLINA
            South Caroliniana Library
            Columbia, S.C.   29208
            (803) 777-5183
      Hours: 8:30-5 M-F.
             8:30-1 Sat.
      Access: By permission.
      Copying facilities.
Sources:
Courtenay Family Papers, 1880-1963; William Dickson, 1739-
1820, A Genealogy; Earle and Birney Families, 1896-1977;
Edgeworth Family, 1781-1870; Kincaid-Anderson Families, 1767
-1926; Davison McDowell, 1784-1842, 1767-1838; McKenzie Family,
1831-1945; Moore-Gillespie Families, 1800-1893; Obear Family,
1834-1941; Reynolds Family, 1837-1887; and The Leonardo

Andrea Genealogical Collection (1,029 folders of compiled
genealogical information & records on some 825 surnames).
Published finding aids: Allen H. Stokes, Jr., A Guide to the
MS Collection of the South Caroliniana Library (1982).

268.   FURMAN UNIVERSITY LIBRARY
          Special Collections
          Greenville, S.C.   29613
          (803) 294-2194
       Hours: 8:30-4:30 M-F.
       Access: Open.
       Copying facilities.
Sources:
See NUCMC, 1963-66, NHPRC. (Materials, from 1730, relate to
history of Baptists in S.C., include minutes of Baptist Associations and annuals of S.C. Baptist Convention, microfilm
records of S.C. Baptist Churches, biographical files, & files
on individual churches).
Published finding aids: None.

269.   WINTHROP COLLEGE
          Dacus Library Archives
          Rock Hill, S.C.   29733
          (803) 323-2131
       Hours: 8:30-5 M-F.
       Access: On-site use only.
       Copying facilities.
Sources:
Clan Donal Archives (official center USA), 1953-1983, &
catalogue; Clanal C. Clelland Archives; collections of Clan
newsletters for Cunning & Hunter Collections of Clan Society
of USA newsletters; Scotch-Irish Heritage Festivals I & II
(1980 & '83) Records (unpublished papers, correspondence, &
audial tapes); York County Multi-Ethnic Heritage Project Records, 1977 (video cassette tapes, slides, posters, trans-
parencies, & newspaper clippings); a genealogical collection
(wills, deeds, land grants, personal letters, and papers);
family papers of settlers in the Piedmont of S.C.; area
Presbyterian church histories & related records, volumes of
tombstone inscriptions, clippings & pamphlet files.
Published finding aids: Winthrop College Archives & Special
Collections: A Guide (W.C., n.d.).

270.   YORK COUNTY LIBRARY
          138 East Black
          Rock Hill, S.C.   29730
          (803) 324-3055
       Hours: 9-9 M-Th.
              9-6 F-Sat.
       Access: On-site use only.
       Copying facilities.
Sources:
The library has an extensive collection of family histories,
church histories, and volumes of tombstone inscriptions,
personal memoirs, diaries, & maps from 1760, land grants,
newspaper clippings, card file of family names.

Published finding aids: None.

271. WOFFORD COLLEGE ARCHIVES
          Spartanburg, S.C.   29301
          (803) 585-4821
      Hours: 9-5 M-F.
      Access: Open.
      Copying facilities.
Sources:
Materials, from 1795, include records of the Historical
Society of S.C. Conference of the United Methodist Church
(minutes, reports, journals, letters, & other papers).
Published finding aids: None.

SOUTH DAKOTA

272. DAKOTAH PRAIRIE MUSEUM
          21 South Main Street/ P.O. Box 395
          Aberdeen, S.D.   57401
          (605) 229-1608
      Hours: 9-5 M-F.
             1-4 Sat., Sun.
      Access: By appointment.
      Copying facilities.
Sources:
Materials, from 1797, relate to northeastern South Dakota,
include ledgers, school records, oral histories, organizational records, and letters & manuscripts. (See Welsh Set-
lement in Brown County in Early History of Brown County, S.D.
1970).

273. SOUTH DAKOTA ARCHIVES RESOURCE CENTER OF S.D. DEPT. OF
      EDUCATION & CULTURAL AFFAIRS
          Records Management Building
          East Truck Bypass
          Pierre, S.D.   57501
          (605) 224-3173
      Hours: 8-5 M-F.
      Access: Open.
      Copying facilities.
Sources:
State & local government records, primarily after 1900.
Published finding aids: None.

274. SOUTH DAKOTA HISTORICAL RESOURCE CENTER
          Soldiers Memorial Building
          Pierre, S.D.   57501
          (605) 224-3615
      Hours: 8-5 M-F.
      Access: Open.
      Copying facilities.
Sources:

County histories, atlases east of the Missouri River, state
newspapers, S.D. census cards, 1905-1945; Federal Census on
film, 1860-1880, 1900, 1910; biographical accounts, genealogical collections, some manuscripts. (Collection held jointly
with the S.D. State Historical Society, listed below).
Published finding aids: None.

275.   SOUTH DAKOTA STATE HISTORICAL SOCIETY
           Memorial Building
           Pierre, S.D.   57501
           (605) 773-3615
       Hours: 8-5 M-F.
       Access: Open, but supervised.
       Copying facilities.
Sources:
(Collection hled jointly with the S.D. Historical Resource
Center; see previous entry).
Published finding aids: None.

276.   UNIVERSITY OF SOUTH DAKOTA, I.D. WEEKS LIBRARY
           Richardson Archives
           Vermillion, S.D.   57069
           (605) 677-5371
       Hours: 8-12m M-F.
              10-5   Sat.
              2-12m Sun.
       Access: Open.
       Copying facilities.
Sources:
Materials, from 1860, include papers of prominent S.D. citi-
zens, records of WPA & Federal Writers Project.
Published finding aids: None.

TENNESSEE

277.   CHATTANOOGA-HAMILTON COUNTY BICENTENNIAL LIBRARY
           1001 Broad Street
           Chattanooga, TN.   37402-2652
           (615) 757-5312
       Hours: 9-9 M-F
              9-6 Sat.
       Access: Open.
       Copying facilities.
Sources:
Henry Clay Evans Papers, 1888-1908; Tomlinson Fort and Family
Papers, 1839-1910; Jesse T. Hill Papers, 1880-1905; David M.
Key Papers, 1834-1901; Albert S. Lenoir Papers, 1831-1921;
C.L. Loop Papers, 1834-1915; records of city of Chattanooga;
depository for Chattanooga Area Historical Association.
Published finding aids: None.

278. JACKSON-MADISON COUNTY LIBRARY
            433 East Lafayette
            Jackson, TN. 38301
            (901) 423-0225
        Hours: 9:30-9 M-Th.
               9:30-5 F-Sat.
        Access: Open.
        Copying facilities.
Sources:
Materials, from 1850, focus on local & Tenn. history, include
diaries, records of early pioneers & soldiers, church records,
land grants, clipping files, and funeral notices, 1860-
Published finding aids: None.

279. UNIVERSITY OF TENNESSEE AT KNOXVILLE
            James D. Hoskins Library
            Knoxville, TN. 37916-1000
            (615) 974-4465
        Hours: 9-5:30 M-F.
               9-12 noon Sat.
        Access: By permission.
        Copying facilities.
Sources:
William B. Lenoir Family Papers, 1787-1913; Rhea Family,
1835-1931; Mary B. Temple (DAR leader), 1876-1920; Campbell
Wallace Papers, 1840-1946; Rhea County Archives, 1785-1875;
business records, 1813-1927; Historical Records Survey &
others.
Published finding aids: Guide to Collections of MS in Tennessee (HRS, 1975).

280. BLOUNT COUNTY PUBLIC LIBRARY
            301 McGhee Street
            Maryville, TN. 37801
            (615) 982-0981
        Hours: 9-8 M-Th.
               9-5:30 F-Sat.
        Access: Open.
        Copying facilities.
Sources:
Census records, 1830-1910; court records, 1795-1970 (e.g.,
marriages, deeds, wills, estate inventories, tax books);
Parham Papers (vertical file of 500 folders on Blount Co.
families); family records, misc. information on churches,
schools, maps.
Published finding aids: None.

281. MEMPHIS-SHELBY COUNTY PUBLIC LIBRARY & INFORMATION
      CENTER
            1850 Peabody Avenue
            Memphis, TN. 38104
            (901) 528-2961
        Hours: 9-9 M-F.
               9-6 Sat.
        Access: Open.
        Copying facilities.

Sources:
Henry A. Montgomery & Family Papers, 1856-1928; Diary of
Josiah Hinds, 1839-62; Papers of George C. Harris, 1873-79;
papers concerning Illinois Central & other railroads, 1893-
1935; some genealogical records.
Published finding aids: None, but individual aids available
at the library.

282. MEMPHIS STATE UNIVERSITY LIBRARIES
         Memphis, TN. 38152
         (901) 454-2201
    Hours: 8-9 M.
           8-5 T-F.
    Access: Post high school age only.
    Copying facilities.
Sources:
Collections focus on Memphis & lower Mississippi Valley; in-
clude records of individuals & organizations, oral history,
19th & 20th century politics.
Published finding aids: None.

283. TENNESSEE STATE LIBRARY & ARCHIVES
         Archives & MS Section
         403 7th Avenue North
         Nashville, TN. 37215
    Hours: 8-4:30 M.
           12n-4:30 T.
           8-4:30 W-Sat.
    Access: Open.
    Copying facilities.
Sources:
Yeatman-Polk Collection (indexed), 1900-1970 (900 families);
Stickley Collection (English lineage & family information,
900 families); Caroline Clark Crockett Papers, 1867-1959
(450 families); Cooper Family, 1716-1968; Susie Gentry Papers,
1777-1934; McGavock Family, 1820-1939; Scotch-Irish Congress
1899; Tenn. Historical Society misc. records, 1688-1951.
Published finding aids: Indexes to collections.

284. VANDERBILT UNIVERSITY LIBRARY
         419 21st Avenue
         Nashville, TN. 37240-0007
         (615) 322-2834
    Hours: 8-4:30 M-F.
    Access: By permission.
    Copying facilities.
Sources:
Materials, from 1800, focus on social & cultural history of
Tennessee and the South, Antebellum & Civil War ms, univer-
sity archives, Vanderbilt Family Papers.
Published finding aids: None, but individual aids available
at the library.

TEXAS

285. UNIVERSITY OF TEXAS AT ARLINGTON LIBRARY
            Dept. of Special Collections
            Arlington, TX. 76019
            (817) 273-3391
        Hours: 8-5 M-W.
               8-10 Th.
               8-5 F.
               10-4 Sat.
        Access: By permission.
        Copying facilities.
Sources:
NHPRC (Materials, from late 1600's, focus on the history of
Texas, including Mexican War, Sam Houston, Albert S. Johnson,
and the Robertson Colony; also microfilm of State, notarial,
& ecclesiastical archives of Mexican State of Yucatan).
Published finding aids: Hart Cohen, Descriptive Guide to the
Collections (1974).

286. TEXAS STATE LIBRARY
            Archives Division
            P.O. Box 12927, Capitol Station
            Austin, TX. 78711
            (512) 475-2445
        Hours: 8-5 M-F.
        Access: On-site use.
        Copying facilities.
Sources:
"Colonization Records" Secretary of State Record Group,
McMullen & McGloin Colony Papers and Passenger Lists (Irish);
Charles Mercer Colony Papers (English); "Voters Registration
of 1867" (county of birth & naturalization data); "Memorials
& Petitions" (data for McMullen/McGloin & Mercer Colonies);
"Customs House Papers", 1836-45 (ship arrivals, some passenger
lists & ship manifests); "Department of Agriculture, Insurance,
Statistics, & History, Biennial Report, 1888" (provides a
statistical breakdown of ethnicity by county in Texas).
Published finding aids: None.

287. UNIVERSITY OF TEXAS AT AUSTIN
            Barker Texas History Center
            Sid Richardson Hall 2.109
            Austin, TX. 78712
            (512) 471-5961 & 7521
        Hours: 8-5 M-Sat.
        Access: Open.
        Copying facilities.
Sources:
Extensive series of ms collections dating from the 16th cen-
tury, including 18 identified as English, 3 as Irish, and 2
as Scottish; several thousand others relating to the history
of Texas, the American Southwest, and American South, & the
University.
Published finding aids: Chester V. Kielman, ed., Guide to the

Historical Manuscript Collection in the U. of Tex. Library
(U. Tx. P., 1967).

283. DALLAS HISTORICAL SOCIETY LIBRARY & ARCHIVES
            Hall of State, Fair Park/ P.O. Box 26038
            Dallas, TX. 75226
            (214) 421-5136
      Hours: 9-5 M-F.
            Sat., by appointment.
      Access: Application necessary.
      Copying facilities.
Sources:
Materials, from 1590, focus on the history of Texas from the
period of Spanish Central to the present; include Joseph
Weldon Bailey Papers, 1880-1930; William Lewis Cabell, 1849-
1910: Franklin Chase & Wife, 1840-80, and others; also papers
of the Texas Emigration and Land Co., 1834-55; pioneer family
papers; Howard Collection of Mexican-American documents.
Published finding aids: Brochure available from the society.

289. DALLAS PUBLIC LIBRARY
            History of Social Sciences Division
            1515 Young Street
            Dallas, TX. 75201
            (214) 749-4129
      Hours: 9-9 M-Th.
            9-5 F-Sat.
            1-5 Sun.
      Access: Open.
      Copying facilities.
Sources:
Data from early wills, marriage, cemetery & church records
for Dallas & other TX. counties; 25,200 microforms from
National Archives, passenger lists from New Orleans, 1813-
61, & Galveston, and lists for Texas inbound ships, 1895-
1954; all of the printed sources in P. Williams Filby's
Passenger & Immigrations Lists Bibliography 1538-1900 (See
also Texas/Dallas Archives & History Division of the Library).
Published finding aids: None.

290. UNIVERSITY OF TEXAS AT EL PASO LIBRARY
            Dept. of Special Collections & Archives
            El Paso, TX. 79968
            (915) 747-5697
      Hours: 8-5 M-F.
      Access: Open.
      Copying facilities.
Sources:
Hamer, NHPRC (Materials, from 1631, include records of the
El Paso & Northeastern Railway Company, 1897-1905, El Paso
& Southwestern Railroad Company, 1905-24, & Rio Grande Divi-
sion of Southern Pacific Co., 1924-58; microfilm of Mexican
archival records, personal papers & documents, regional de-
pository for city & county records.
Published finding aids: Mildred Torok, The U. of TX. at El
Paso Archives (1972) & R.P. Daguerre, ed., List of Archival

Accessions (1975).

291. FEDERAL ARCHIVES & RECORDS CENTER
            c/o Regional Archivist
            501 West Felix Street/ P.O. Box 6216
            Fort Worth, TX. 76115
            (817) 334-5525
        Hours: 8-4 M-F.
        Access: Most collections open.
        Copying facilities.
Sources:
(Serves AR., LA., N.M., OK., & TX.). Records of District
Courts of U.S. (Civil, Criminal, Admiralty, & Bankruptcy)
until the 1950's; Records of United Court of Appeals, 1891-
1950's; Records of Bureau of Indian Affairs; Records of
Bureau of Customs; Records of Office of the Chief of Engineers;
census records; NARC Microfilms (genealogy/ethnology).
Published finding aids: Research Opportunities (General
Services Administration: National Archives and Records Ser-
vice, 1980).

292. ROSENBERG LIBRARY
            Archives Department
            2310 Sealy
            Galveston, TX. 77550
            (713) 763-8854
        Hours: 10-5 T-Sat.
        Access: Open.
        Copying facilities.
Sources:
Materials, from 1655, relate to the colonization, the Texas
Revolution, The Republic, immigration, and railroad and land
speculation; including Samuel May Williams Papers, 1822-64;
James Morgan, 1809-80; John D. Lockhart, 1830-1918; Ben C.
Stuart, 1870-1921; Henry M. Truehart, 1839-1905; Zebulon L.
White, 1860-89; and others.
Published finding aids: See Day's Handbook (below).

293. RICE UNIVERSITY LIBRARY
            6100 South Main Street/ P.O. Box 1892
            Houston, TX. 77001
            (713) 527-8101
        Hours: 9-4 M-F.
        Access: By permission.
        Copying facilities.
Sources:
Materials, from 1600, focus on Texas history; include James
Stephen Hogg Papers, 1887-1905; Mirafeau Buonaparte Lamar
Journal (Georgia to Texas 1835), and others.
Published finding aids: See J.M. Day's Handbook of Texas
Archival & MS Depositories. (Texas Library & Hist. Commission
Austin, 1966).

294. TEXAS TECH UNIVERSITY
            Southwest Collection
            West Broadway
            Lubbock, TX. 79409

                    (806) 742-3749
              Hours: 8-5 M-F.
                     9-3 Sat.
              Access: Open.
              Copying facilities.
Sources:
Manuscripts, with 19th & 20th century focus, concentrate on
Texas and Southwest; include personal papers of Amos G. Car-
ter, William Curry Holder, Clifford B. Jones, Elijah P. Love-
joy & Carl Coke Rister; business records of Yellow House Land
Company, Texas Land & Developement Co., Spur Ranch, and
others; also, data files on individuals & families.
Published finding aids: See Day's Handbook (above).

295 . STEPHEN F. AUSTIN STATE UNIVERSITY LIBRARY
              Nacogdoches, TX. 75961
              (713) 569-4101
              Hours: 8-5 M-F.
                    10-6 Sat.
              Access: By permission.
              Copying facilities.
Sources:
Collection, from 1812, focuses on East Texas; includes correspondence of Samuel E. Asbury, George Crockett and others;
legal papers and accounts of lawsuits, land grants, deeds,
and land transfers; notes on religion, original writings of
East Texans, records of East Texas lumber, industrial, and
railroad companies.
Published finding aids: Day's Handbook (above).

UTAH

296.   BRIGHAM YOUNG UNIVERSITY
              Harold B. Lee Library
              Archives & MS
              Provo, UT. 84602
              (801) 378-3514
              Hours: 8-5 M-F.
              Access: Interview required.
              Copying facilities.
Sources:
Histories, family collections, diaries, & journals; bulk
relates to Mormon Missionary work in Great Britain after
1840.
Published finding aids: Andrus & Bennett Mormon MS to 1846
(BYUP, 1977), & David Britton, ed., Guide to Mormon Diaries
& Autobiographies (BYUP, 1977), which is indexed.

297.   CHURCH OF JESUS CHRIST OF LATTER-DAY SAINTS
              Genealogical Library
              50 East North Temple
              Salt Lake City, UT. 84150

```
             (801)531-2331
     Hours: 7:30-6  M.
            7:30-10 T-F.
            7:30-5  Sat.
     Access: Open.
     Copying facilities.
```

Sources:
Of the 900,000+ reels of microfilm, nearly 100,000 are devoted
to the British Collection (i.e., records in the four countries
of this directory); The American Collection furnishes many
other reels devoted to the U.S.A. & Canada. All include family
histories, many giving immigration details. American Collection includes passenger lists for most Atlantic & Gulf posts.
Published finding aids: Arlene H. Eakle, et. al., Descriptive
Inventory of the English Collection (UUP, 1979) & Ronald
Cunningham, A Handy Guide to the Genealogical Library & Church
Historical Department (Logan: Everton, 1981).

298 .   CHURCH OF JESUS CHRIST OF LATTER-DAY SAINTS
                Historical Department
                50 East North Temple
                Salt Lake City, UT. 84150
        Hours: 8-4:30 M-Sat.
        Access: Interview required.
        Copying facilities.
Sources:
NHPRC (Materials, from 1880, include the Archives of the
Morman Church, records of 15,000+ local churches, minutes of
meetings, & financial & membership records; more than 5,000
ms collections include journals & diaries, & records of church
related organizations).
Published finding aids: See Cunningham's Handy Guide (previous entry).

299 .   UNIVERSITY OF UTAH
                Marriott Library, MS Division
                Salt Lake, UT. 84112
                (801) 581-8863
        Hours: 8-5 M-F.
        Access: Some 2% of Collection restricted.
        Copying facilities.
Sources:
Hiram B. Clawson Papers, Autobiography of Zodak Knapp Judd,
Gustive O. Larson Papers (statistical data on immigration),
Records of the Utah Humanities Research Foundation, Nelphi
L. Morris Papers, Madeline R. McQuown Papers, & A. Russell
Mortensen Papers.
Published finding aids: A register for each of the above
collections.

300 .   UTAH STATE ARCHIVES RESEARCH CENTER
                2333 South 2300 West
                Salt Lake City, UT. 84119
                (801) 533-4273
        Hours: 8-5 M-F.
        Access: Restrictions on Medical records, Security
```
```

Commission, Adoptions, & Prisons files.
Copying facilities.
Sources:
Materials, from 1850, include all official records of the
Territory, the State, and all counties.
Published finding aids: Guide to Utah State Archives (1977),
Guide to Official Records of Genealogical Value in the State
of Utah (on fiche, 1980), & others.

301.. UTAH STATE HISTORICAL SOCIETY
        300 Rio Grande
        Salt Lake City, UT. 84101
        (801) 533-5808
        Hours: 8-5 M-F.
        Access: By permission.
        Copying facilities.
Sources:
NHPRC & Hamer. (Materials, from 1830, relate to the exploration, settlement, & development of Utah, & to the history of
the Mormon Church; includes diaries, journals, reminiscences,
& letters; files of WPA Writers Project & Historical Records
Survey).
Published finding aids: Registers to individual collections
are available.

VERMONT

302 . CASTLETON STATE COLLEGE LIBRARY
        Castleton, VT. 05735
        (802) 468-5611
(Not in NHPRC, Hamer, or NUCMC; no response to questionnaire).

303. VERMONT DEPARTMENT OF LIBRARIES
        Law & Documents Unit
        111 State Street
        Montpelier, VT. 05602
        (802) 828-3261
        Hours: 8-4:30 M-F.
        Access: Open.
        Copying facilities.
Sources:
Manuscript censuses of Vermont, 1790-1880.
Published finding aids: None.

304. VERMONT HISTORICAL SOCIETY LIBRARY
        Pavilion Building
        Montpelier, VT. 05602
        (802) 828-2291
        Hours: 8-5:30 M-F.
        Access: Open; non-circulating.
        Copying facilities.
Sources:

State and local history for VT. & rest of New England, Upper
New York & Lower Canada; personal papers of Jonathan Hubbard,
1809-51; Oliver Johnson, 1861-89; Justin S. Morrill, 1828-96,
and others; business papers connected to land, canal, & railroad; school records, church records, town records, genealogical collection includes Whitelaw Papers (documents Scottish
settlement in Ryegate).
Published finding aids: A Guide to the Vermont Historical
Society Library (1981).

305. VERMONT PUBLIC RECORDS DIVISION
            Agency of Administration
            6 Baldwin Street
            Montpelier, VT. 05602
            (802) 828-3288
      Hours: 8-4 M-F.
      Access: Open.
      Copying facilities.
Sources:
NHPRC (Materials focus on post-1900 State Records; include
town & county records, vital statistics, church records,
probate records).
Published finding aids: None.

306. VERMONT STATE PAPERS DIVISION
            Secretary of State's Office
            Pavilion Building
            109 State Street
            Montpelier, VT. 05602
            (802) 828-2397
      Hours: 7:45-4:30 M-F.
      Access: Open.
      Copying facilities.
Sources:
Archives of State chiefly prior to 1900, federal/state/county
records, governmental correspondence, deeds, leases, agreements, etc.; Rutland, Chittendon, Bennington, & Windham Co.,
and Barre City court naturalizations; pamphlets dealing with
Irish riots & Scottish petitions.
Published finding aids: Inventories for some collections; all
indexed in catalogue of cards.

307. GREEN MOUNTAIN COLLEGE LIBRARY
            Poultney, VT. 05764
            (802) 287-9313
      Hours: 8-5 M-F.
            6:30-10:30 p.m. M-Th.
            1-5 Sat. & Sun.
      Access: Open.
      Copying facilities.
Sources:
Welsh Collection Room (1200 bound volumes) and immigrant
card file, listing names and place of origin.
Published finding aids: None.

VIRGIN ISLANDS

308. VIRGIN ISLANDS
(See National Archives in Washington, D.C. and Federal
Archives and Records Center, Bayonne N.J.; also, George F.
Tyson & Carolyn Tyson's Preliminary Report on MS Materials
in British Archives Relating to the American Revolution in
the West Indian Islands, 1974. Not listed in Hamer or NUCMC.
Queries to NHPRC identified sources - Florence A. Williams
Public Library, St. Croix; Island Resources Foundation, St.
Thomas; & Virgin Isle Bureau of Libraries & Museums, St.
Thomas - indicate few immigration records and related mater-
ials are available in the islands.

VIRGINIA

309. VIRGINIA POLYTECHNIC INSTITUTE & STATE UNIVERSITY
         Library Special Collections
         Blacksburg, VA.   24061
         (703) 951-6308
      Hours: 8-5 M-F.
      Access: By permission.
      Copying facilities.
Sources:
NHPRC (Materials, from 1830, include business papers, account
books, and political papers from Southwestern VA.).
Published finding aids: None.

310. UNIVERSITY OF VIRGINIA LIBRARIES
         MS & Archives
         Charlottesville, VA.   22901
         (804) 924-3025
      Hours: 9-5 M-F.
             9-1 Sat.
      Access: Identification required.
      Copying facilities.
Sources:
NUCMC, 1959-65, '67, '69, '71-72, '74; NHPRC, Hamer. (Mater-
ials, from 1650, relate to the history of Virginia & the
Southeastern U.S.; include papers of presidents, cabinet
members, members of Congress, Justices of the U.S. Supreme
Court, other public officials, military leaders, clergymen).

311. VIRGINIA MILITARY INSTITUTE LIBRARY
         Lexington, VA.   24450
         (703) 463-6228
      Hours: 9-5 M-F.
      Access: By permission.
      Copying facilities.
Sources:
NUCMC, 1959-61, '64; Hamer. (Materials include the Stonewall
Jackson Collection of letters & ms.).
Published finding aids: None.

312. WASHINGTON & LEE UNIVERSITY
            Special Collections
            Lexington, VA. 24450
            (703) 463-9111
      Hours: 9-5 M-F.
      Access: Scholars only.
      Copying facilities.
Sources:
NHPRC, NUCMC, 1963, Hamer. (Materials, from 1750, relate to
Lexington & Rochbridge families, 1780-1900).
Published finding aids: Guide to MS at Cyrus Hall McCormick
Library, Washington & Lee (1976).

313. MARINER'S MUSEUM LIBRARY
            Newport News, VA. 23606
            (804) 595-0368
      Hours: 9-5 M-Sat.
      Access: Open.
      Copying facilities.
Sources:
NHPRC, NUCMC, 1959-61, Hamer. (Materials, from 1776, include
numerous ships logbooks & account books, and several hundred
letters; also, specifications, contracts, etc.).
Published finding aids: Catalog of Maps, Ships' Papers and
Logbooks, The Mariners Museum Library (G.K. Hall, 1964).

314. OLD DOMINION UNIVERSITY LIBRARY
            Norfolk, VA. 23508
            (804) 489-6610
      Hours: 8-5 M-F.
      Access: By permission.
      Copying facilities.
Sources:
NHPRC (Materials, from 1794, include papers of 8 prominent
citizens of Norfolk). See also, the Scottish Collection of
books & manuscripts.
Published finding aids: None.

315. UNION THEOLOGICAL SEMINARY IN VIRGINIA LIBRARY
            3401 Brook Road
            Richmond, VA. 23227
            (804) 355-0671
      Hours: 8:30-5 M-F.
      Access: By permission.
      Copying facilities.
Sources:
Hamer, NUCMC, 1971, NHPRC. (Materials, from 1750, relate to
the Presbyterian Church in the U.S., especially the Virginias/
North Carolina - include synod minutes, session minutes,
marriage & baptismal records of a few churches, some diaries
& letters).
Published finding aids: None.

316.   VIRGINIA BAPTIST HISTORICAL SOCIETY
            Box 95, University of Richmond
            Richmond, VA.   23173
            (804) 285-6852
See Hamer (Records of VA. Baptist Churches, 1762-1959, in-
cluding diaries, sermons, letters, minutes).
Questionnaire not returned.

317.   VIRGINIA HISTORICAL SOCIETY LIBRARY
            Boulevard at Kensington/ P.O. Box 7311
            Richmond, VA.   23221
            (804) 358-4901
        Hours: 9-5 M-F.
        Access: Identification required.
        Copying facilities.
Sources:
Materials, from 1607, relate to Virginia and the South.
Emigration materials include Beverley Family Papers, 1654-
1929; Cobell Family Papers, 1774-1941; Dabney Family Papers,
1742-1928; Mason Family Papers, 1813-1943; Minor Family
Papers, 1810-1932; and others, including disparate letters.
Published finding aids: None.

318.   VIRGINIA STATE LIBRARY
            Archives Division
            11th & Capitol Streets
            Richmond, VA.   23219-3491
            (804) 786-8929
        Hours: 8:15-5 M-Sat.
        Access: By permission.
Sources:
Records of state government, copies of County Court records
(i.e., wills, deeds, orders, & marriage bonds to 1865), some
church records, some personal papers, unpublished genealogical notes, & Bible records; indexed by county.
Published finding aids: (pamphlet) Genealogical Research in
the Virginia State Library (VSL, n.d.).

319.   COLONIAL WILLIAMSBURG FOUNDATION
            Research Archives
            Francis & South Henry Street/ Drawer O
            Williamsburg, VA.   23185
            (804) 229-1000
        Hours: 9-5 M-F.
        Access: By permission.
        Copying facilities.
Sources:
NHPRC, NUCMC, 1959-62, 68, Hamer. (Materials, from 1600, in-
clude account books, business, personal & family papers, and
other manuscripts dealing with British Colonies; micro-film
copies of American & British ms which relate to VA.).
Published finding aids: Marylee G. McGregor, Guide to the
MS Collections of Colonial Williamsburg (1969).

320.. WILLIAM & MARY COLLEGE LIBRARY
          Williamsburg, VA. 23185
          (804) 253-4404
      Hours: 8-5 M-F.
             9-1 Sat.
      Access: By permission.
      Copying facilities.
Sources:
NHPRC, NUCMC 1966, Hamer. (Materials, from 1650, focus on
the Colonial & early national period of Virginia history;
include diaries, account books, letters, & other documents).
Published finding aids: None.

WASHINGTON

321 . STATE CAPITOL HISTORICAL ASSOCIATION
          211 West 21st Avenue
          Olympia, WA. 98501
Questionnaire not returned; see Hamer. (MS, from 1846, relate
to the settlement & development of the state; include pioneer
papers & papers of churches and schools).

322 . WASHINGTON STATE ARCHIVES
          12th & Washington Streets/ P.O. Box 9000
          Olympia, WA. 98504
          (206) 754-1492
      Hours: 8-5 M-F.
      Access: Privacy restrictions as per state law.
      Copying facilities.
Sources:
Materials, from 1851, are state & local government records
only. These include territorial census rolls, naturalization
records, & military records, birth & death index (1907-59),
burial records, and professional licensing records. Query
for list of specialized publications.
Published finding aids: General Guide to the Washington State
Archives (1969).

323 . WASHINGTON STATE LIBRARY
          Olympia, WA. 98504
          (206) 753-5590
      Hours: 8-5 M-F.
      Access: Open.
      Copying facilities.
Sources:
Hamer, NUCMC, 1959, NHPRC. (Materials, from 1837, include
government records, interviews w/ pioneers, & collections of
pioneer letters & records).
Published finding aids: Historical Records of Washington
State: Records & Papers Held at Repositories (WSHR, 1981).

324. WASHINGTON STATE UNIVERSITY LIBRARY
         MS, Archives, & Special Collections
         Pullman, WA. 99164-5610
         (509) 335-6691
     Hours: 8-5 M-F.
     Access: Open.
Sources:
Nicholas D'Arcy Estate Papers, 1791-1869 (marriage agreements,
land title documents, maps, genealogical notes, & other papers
regarding transfer of lands in County Roscommon, Ireland).
Published finding aids: Selected MS Resources in the Washington State University Library (WSU, 1974).

325. FEDERAL ARCHIVES AND RECORDS CENTER
         c/o Regional Archivist
         6125 Sand Point Way NE.
         Seattle, WA. 98115
         (206) 526-6507
     Hours: 7:45-4:15 M-F.
     Access: Most collections open.
     Copying facilities.
Sources:
(Serves AK., IA., OR., & WA.). Records of District Courts of
U.S. (Civil, Criminal, Admiralty, & Bankruptcy) until the
1950's; Records of United Courts of Appeals, 1891-1950's;
Records of Bureau of Indian Affairs; Bureau of Customs Re-
cords; Records of Office of the Chief of Engineers; census
records; NARC Microfilms (genealogy/ethnology); Records of
Office of Governor of Alaska, 1884-1958; Records of U.S.
Commission for U.S. Science Exhibit at Seattle World's Fair,
1956-63; Papers of Sir Henry Wellcome, 1856-1936.
Published finding aids: Research Opportunities (General Services Administration: National Archives and Records Service,
1980).

326. SEATTLE HISTORICAL SOCIETY ARCHIVES
         216 East Hamlin
         Seattle, WA. 98112
         (206) 324-1125
     Hours: 11-5 T-F.
            10-3 Sat.
     Access: By appointment.
     Copying facilities.
Sources:
NHPRC (Materials, from 1851, include ships logbooks & data
on Seattle pioneers; focus on Seattle, King County, Alaska,
& Western Washington, in that order).
Published finding aids: None.

327. UNIVERSITY OF WASHINGTON LIBRARIES
         MS Collection
         Seattle, WA. 98195
         (206) 543-1879
     Hours: 8-12 & 1-5 M-F.
     Access: Most materials open to the public.
Sources:

Materials, ms, from 1812, include Clarence Booth Bagley Papers
1861-1932, & his frontier collection, 1854-89; David Edward
Blaine Letters, 1849-62; James G. Swan Papers & Diaries, 1859
-98; William Henson Wallace Papers; and others. Some materials
describe overland crossings to the Pacific Northwest. State-
hood period is also well represented by collections. See also,
Alaska & British Columbia Collection, 1866-1948, and Hudson
Bay Papers, 1834-70.
Published finding aids: Comprehensive Guide to the MS Collections & to the Personal Papers in the University Archives.
(UWL, 1984).

328. TACOMA PUBLIC LIBRARY
            1102 Tacoma Avenue South
            Tacoma, WA. 98402-2098
            (206) 591-5666
        Hours: 9-9 M-F.
               9-6 Sat.
        Access: Open.
        Copying facilities.
Sources:
NUCMC, 1970-72, 74; NHPRC. (Materials, from 1850, include
Northern Pacific Railroad papers, records of Tacoma busines-
ses and organizations, papers of local people, large photo
collection, and oral history).
Published finding aids: None.

329. WASHINGTON STATE HISTORICAL SOCIETY
            315 North Stadium Way
            Tacoma, WA. 98403
            (205) 593-2830
        Hours: 11-5 T-F.
               10-3 Sat.
        Access: By permission.
        Copying facilities.
Sources:
NUCMC, 1970, Hamer. (Materials, from 1790, include court,
county, city archives; church records, diaries & papers des-
cribing overland crossings & pioneer settlement, & correspondence of missionaries).

WEST VIRGINIA

(For Pre-Civil War materials, see also Virginia repositories).

330. WEST VIRGINIA DEPT. OF ARCHIVES & HISTORY
            Capitol Complex
            Charleston, W.V. 25305
            (304) 348-2277
        Hours: 9-5 M-F.
        Access: Open.
        Copying facilities.

Sources:
Hamer, NUCMC, 1959, NHPRC. (Materials, from 1729, include state and local government papers, Temperance Society Papers, records of several Methodist & Baptist churches, courthouse records, and records of some VA. agencies).
Published finding aids: None.

331.   MARSHALL UNIVERSITY SPECIAL COLLECTIONS
           Huntington, W.V.   25705
           (304) 696-2320
       Hours: 8-10 M-Th.
              8-4:3- F.
              9-5 Sat.
              1-10 Sun.
       Access: Open.
       Copying facilities.
Sources:
NHPRC (Materials, from the late 1700's, relate to the history of W.V., OH., & KY.; include diaries, letters, business records, oral histories, & interviews).
Published finding aids: None.

332.   MORGANTOWN PUBLIC LIBRARY
           West Virginia Collection & Archives
           373 Spruce Street
           Morgantown, W.V.   26505
           (304) 296-1759
       Hours: 10-9 M-F.
              10-5 Sat.
              1-6 Sun.
       Access: Open.
       Copying facilities.
Sources:
NHPRC (Materials, from 1820's, include the Moreland Collection of diaries, letters, & other manuscripts; Morgantown history, and genealogical data).
Published finding aids: None.

333.   WEST VIRGINIA UNIVERSITY LIBRARY
           Colson Hall
           Morgantown, W.V.   26506
           (304) 293-3536
       Hours: 8:15-5 M-F.
              8:30-12:30 Sat.
       Access: By permission.
       Copying facilities.
Sources:
NHPRC, Hamer, NUCMC, 1959. (Materials, from 1736, relate to the history of the state, the university, Upper Ohio Valley, Appalachia, coal industry, & organized labor; include Charles Henry Ambler Papers, 1834-1945; Jonathan M. Bennett Papers, 1785-1899; business records of store, stage line, hotel, telegraph company, bank, & canal co.; records of churches & schools).
Published finding aids: James W. Hess, Guide to MS & Archives in the West Virginia Collection (1974).

WISCONSIN

334. UNIVERSITY OF WISCONSIN AT EAU CLAIRE
          Archives & Area Research Center
          Eau Claire, WI.   54701
          (715) 836-2739
      Hours: 1-5 M-F.
      Access: Open.
      Copying facilities.
Sources:
NUCMC, 1968, NHPRC (Materials, from 1837, document local history in the region this center represents; included are
business & government records, labor union records, and records of social groups).
Published finding aids: None current.

335. STATE HISTORICAL SOCIETY OF WISCONSIN
          816 State Street
          Madison, WI.   53706
          (608) 262-9576
      Hours: 8-5 M-F.
             9-4 Sat.
      Access: Present identification.
      Copying facilities.
Sources:
Joseph P. O'Donnell Papers, 1847-1906; Michael Brady Diary,
1842-52; Charles & Mary Stewart Papers, 1849-1923; William
Cross Diary, 1831; Isabella McKinnon Diary, 1852; George F.
Shepperd Papers, 1857-1901; Owen Family Correspondence, 1847-
63, 1907-12; and others. See also typescripts of "Irish in
Wisconsin", "English in Wisconsin", "Scots in Wisconsin", &
"Welsh in Wisconsin".
Published finding aids: David J. Delgado, Guide to the Wis-
consin State Archives (1966), and others.

336. UNIVERSITY OF WISCONSIN AT MADISON LIBRARY
          Manuscripts Dept.
          728 State Street
          Madison, WI.   53706
          (608) 262-3521
      Hours: 9-5 M-F.
      Access: By permission.
      Copying facilities.
Sources:
Hamer (as "University of Wisconsin Memorial Library").
(Materials, from 1772, include William English Walling Papers,
1900-36, and some English manor rolls of 14th & 15th century).
Published finding aids: None.

337. MARQUETTE UNIVERSITY
          Dept. of Special Collections
          1415 W. Wisconsin Avenue
          Milwaukee, WI.   53233
          (414) 224-7256
      Hours: 9-12 & 1-5 M-F.

Access: Open, but query first.
Copying facilities.
Sources:
Catholic Missions to American Indians, 1888 - ; Michael
Collins Papers, 1905-1908; Raphael N. Hamilton Notes; Madonna
Center Papers, 1900-1905; North American French Regime Docu-
ments, 1704-1763.
Published finding aids: J.A. Fleckner & S. Mallach, Guide to
Historical Resources in Milwaukee Area Archives (Milwaukee
Area Archives Group, 1976).

338. MILWAUKEE PUBLIC LIBRARY
            814 W. Wisconsin Avenue
            Milwaukee, WI. 53233
            (414) 278-3000
            Hours: 12:30-9 M.
                12:30-5:15 T-Sat.
            Access: Open.
            Copying facilities.
Sources:
Materials, from 1800, relate to the city, state, and surrounding states, and the Great Lakes; include newspaper microfilm
collection, county property records, theatre records, records
of an insurance and lumber company (ca. 1885-1920), and records of the Republican County Committee, 1893-1904.
Published finding aids: Fleckner & Mallach's Guide (See #338).

339. UNIVERSITY OF WISCONSIN AT MILWAUKEE LIBRARY
            2311 East Hartford Avenue/ P.O. Box 604
            Milwaukee, WI. 53201
            (414) 963-4785
            Hours: 8-4:30 M-F.
            Access: By permission.
            Copying facilities.
Sources:
NUCMC, 1968, NHPRC. (Materials, from 1792, document local
history for this Area Research Center; include government
documents for city, area, & state, as well as personal &
business papers, the University archives, and some literary
collections).
Published finding aids: Fleckner & Mallach, Guide (See #338).

340. WAUKESHA COUNTY HISTORICAL MUSEUM
            Research Center
            101 W. Main Street
            Waukesha, WI. 53186
            (414) 548-7186
            Hours: 9-4:30 M-F.
            Access: Adult on-site use only.
            Copying facilities.
Sources:
Naturalization papers, 1847-1955, for Waukesha Co. (includes
Declaration of Intention); letters, diaries, family papers,
land records, & Civil War Papers; transcripts of birth, death,
and marriage records, tombstone inscriptions & cemetery records, some church records; federal & state census reports

for the county, 1836-95; county histories, local histories,
genealogy notebooks, Pioneer notebooks, typescript essays on
English, Welsh, Scots, and Irish in the county.
Published finding aids: <u>Museum Research Guides</u> (especially
#1, "Primary Bibliography for Research in Waukesha County").

WYOMING

341. WYOMING STATE ARCHIVES, MUSEUMS, & HISTORICAL DEPT.
         Barrett Building
         Cheyenne, WY. 82002
         (307) 777-7020
     Hours: 8-5 M-F.
     Access: Some collections restricted.
     Copying facilities.
Sources:
Original records of state & county governments, 1869-1958;
historical materials, 1865-1960, including diaries, pioneer
narratives, private papers, ledgers, & unpublished ms, name
& general subject card file; Annals of Wyoming; WPA Collec-
tion, census records, microfilm from National Archives on
Wyoming's early military posts, oral history collection.
Published finding aids: <u>WPA Collections Guide</u> (n.d.); <u>Oral
History Guide</u> (n.d.).

342 . UNIVERSITY OF WYOMING LIBRARY
         Special Collections
         Laramie, WY. 82071
         (307) 766-4114
     Hours: 8-5 M-F.
     Access: Open.
     Copying facilities.
Sources:
Hamer, NUCMC, 1966, NHPRC. (Materials, from 1762, include
records of Carter & Sweetwater Counties, 1868-93; a Fort
Laramie Collection, 1868-1900; Wyoming Stockgrowers Association, 1873-1921; Union Pacific Railroad Collection; and
other business-related papers; genealogical materials relate
to the Cranch Family of Massachusetts, including John Adams).
Published finding aids: None.

343. YELLOWSTONE NATIONAL PARK ARCHIVES
         Yellowstone, WY. 82190
         (307) 344-7381
     Hours: 8-4:30 M-F.
     Access: Open.
     Copying facilities.
Sources:
NHPRC (Materials, from 1872, are administrative records,
station logs, scout diaries, reports & correspondence - some
77,000 pages before 1916; identifies Scots, Irish, & English
traders, trappers, & visitors. NO published finding aids.

Canadian Records and Manuscript Repositories

(For an exhaustive list, see <u>Directory of Canadian Records</u> <u>and Manuscript Repositories</u>, Ottawa: Association of Canadian Archivists, 1977; and the <u>Union List of Serials</u> (H.W. Wilson Co., 1965), <u>New Serials Titles</u> (R.R. Bowker Co., 1973), and <u>New Serials Titles</u> (Library of Congress, 1976, 1981, 1984), and <u>Union List of Manuscripts in Canadian Repositories</u>, (Ottawa, 1975) & <u>Supplements</u> (1976, 1978, 1980).

ALBERTA

346. ANGLICAN CHURCH OF CANADA, DIOCESE OF CALGARY, ARCHIVES
         c/o Anglican Cathedral
         602 1st Street, N.E.
         Calgary, Alb. T2G 4W4
         (403) 269-2906
      Hours: 9-4 M-F.
      Access: Open.
      Copying facilities.
Sources:
DCRMR (Records of Calgary Diocese, from 1880, include parish files & records).
Published finding aids: None.

347. PROVINCIAL ARCHIVES OF ALBERTA
         12845 102 Avenue
         Edmonton, Alb. T5N 0M6
         (403) 427-1750
      Hours: 9-4:30 M,T,Th., & F.
             9-9   W.
      Access: Open.
      Copying facilities.
Sources:
Records of the government, religious archives (United Church of Canada, includes Methodist & Presbyterian) prior to 1925, private papers, maps, & photos; Homestead Records, 1885-1930.
Published finding aids: Inventories only.

348. UNITED CHURCH OF CANADA, ALBERTA CONFERENCE ARCHIVES
        St. Stephen's College
        8830 112 Street
        Edmonton, Alb. TOG 2JG
        (403) 439-7311
        Hours: 1-4:30 M-F.
        Access: Open.
        Copying facilities.
Sources:
DCRMR (Registers of baptisms, marriages, and deaths for local
churches).
Published finding aids: None.

BRITISH COLUMBIA

349. KAMLOOPS MUSEUM
        207 Seymour Street
        Kamloops, B.C. V2C 2E7
        (604) 372-9931
        Hours: Winter: 3-5, & 7-11 pm M-F.
                       10-5 Sat.
               Summer: 10-11 M-F.
                       10-5 Sat.
        Access: By appointment only.
Sources:
DCRMR (Hudson Bay Company Records, 1841-1880; indexed news-
papers, 1880-1945; city assessment rolls, 1894-1937; letters,
diaries, ledgers, maps).
Published finding aids: Inventories only.

350. ANGLICAN PROVINCIAL SYNOD OF B.C. ARCHIVES
        6050 Chancellor Blvd.
        Vancouver, B.C. V6T 1X3
        (604) 228-9031
        Hours: 9-12 & 1-4 T-Th.
        Access: Only two items restricted.
        Copying facilities.
Sources:
Diary & other papers of Rt. Rev. George Hills (first Anglican
Bishop of B.C., 1859-95); English Missionary Society Reports
Home (includes those in Canada); Sunday School Caravan Re-
ports; material on miners from Cornwall, 1850-on; Student ms
with references to new settlers; other biographical materials.
Published finding aids: Inventories only.

351. IRVING HOUSE HIST. CENTER & NEW WESTMINSTER MUSEUM
        302 Royal Avenue
        Vancouver, B.C. V3L 1H7
        (604) 521-7656
        Hours: Oct.-Apr. W-F, by appointment only.
               May.-Sept. 11-5 T-Sat.
        Access: Query first.

Copying facilities.
Sources:
DCRMR (Family histories, private papers, maps, & newspapers relating to the area & town).
Published finding aids: None.

350. UNITED CHURCH OF CANADA, B.C. CONFERENCE ARCHIVES
90 Vancouver School of Theology
6000 Iona Drive
Vancouver, B.C.   V6T 1L4
(604) 228-9031
Hours: 10-5 W., & by appointment.
Access: Query first.
Copying facilities.
Sources:
DCRMR (Records, papers, clippings; congregational, institutional, & clergy records of the United Church and its predecessors).
Published finding aids: None.

351. UNIVERSITY OF BRITISH COLUMBIA, SPECIAL COLLECTIONS
2075 Wesbrook Mall
Vancouver, B.C.   V6T 1W5
(604) 228-2521
Hours: 8:30-5 M-F.
9-5   Sat. (Term and Summer only).
Access: By permission.
Copying facilities.
Sources:
DCRMR (University papers & records, private papers, maps, photos).
Published finding aids: None.

352. VANCOUVER CITY ARCHIVES
1150 Chestnut Street
Vancouver, B.C.   V6J 1S5
(604) 736-8561 or 736-8562
Hours: 10-6 M-F.
Access: Open.
Copying facilities.
Sources:
DCRMR (City records, private & business papers, maps, newspaper clippings, and reference materials).
Published finding aids: None.

353. PROVINCIAL ARCHIVES OF BRITISH COLUMBIA
655 Bellerville Street
Victoria, B.C.   V8V 1X4
(604) 387-3621
Hours: 8:30-5 M-F. & by appointment.
Access: Query.
Copying facilities.
Sources:
Government records; Dingle Family Papers, 1893-1960; J. Gordon Smith Papers, ca. 1900-1940; O'Reilly Family, 1795-1963; Hayward Family Records (undertakers), 1862-1963; Gilley Family

Records, 1791-1869; Samuel Black Diaries, Journals, & Papers, 1823-35; other private papers; business & organizational papers.
Published finding aids: Manuscript Inventory No. 1 (1976), Manuscript Inventory No. 2 (1978), and Manuscript Inventory No. 3 (1980).

354. VICTORIA CITY ARCHIVES
        613 Pandora Avenue
        Victoria, B.C.   V8W 1P6
        (604) 385-5711
        Hours: By appointment only.
        Access: Query first.
Sources:
DCRMR (City reports, 1883 to date; city assessment records, private papers, diaries, business records, maps).
Published finding aids: None.

MANITOBA

355. THE HUDSON'S BAY ARCHIVES
        200 Vaughan Street
        Winnipeg, Man.   R3C 0V8
        (204) 943-0881
        Hours: By appointment.
        Access: Reference only.
        Copying facilities.
Sources:
Manitoba Genealogical Society Pamphlet, "Reference Sources for Searching Family History in Manitoba" (Records document the history of the Hudson Bay Company; include fifty-six volumes of account books for Red River Settlement, 1811-71; land registers, Red River census for 1827, and, indexed, a register of baptisms, marriages, & burials, 1821-51, wills of employees & relations, and biographies of fur traders).
Published finding aids: Directory of Archives in Manitoba (Winnipeg, n.d.).

356. THE LEGISLATIVE LIBRARY OF MANITOBA
        200 Vaughan Street
        Winnipeg, Man.   R3C 0V8
        (204) 944-3784
        Hours: By appointment.
        Access: Reference only.
        Copying facilities.
Sources:
MGSP (Listed above in #356). (Focus on provincial government materials, includes vertical file on notable families & current scrapbook of all born in the province before 1895; fairly complete set of newspapers and Henderson's Directories).
Published finding aids: Directory of Archives in Manitoba (Winnipeg, n.d.).

357 . PROVINCIAL ARCHIVES OF MANITOBA
        200 Vaughan Street
        Winnipeg, Man. R3C 0V8
        (204) 946-7252 or 7253
     Hours: 8:30-5 M-F.
     Access: Some restricted materials.
     Copying facilities.
Sources:
Government documents include the Red River Settlement (prior
to 1870) and those for the Province; Pre-1870 records include
census returns for 1831; some parish registers from Anglican,
Presbyterian, & Roman Catholic churches; newspapers; personal
papers, such as the Selkirk Collection; court records. Post
-1870 records include census reports; city & rural directories from 1876; municipal records including voting lists from
1875; Muster Rolls from 1871; individual Scots & Irish papers;
business records; Dept. of Education reports, 1915-65 (gives
pupils names); ships-passenger lists from Halifax & Quebec,
1870-1908.
Published finding aids: Directory of Archives in Manitoba
(Winnipeg, n.d.).

358 . UNITED CHURCH OF CANADA
        Manitoba Conference Archives
        c/o The Library
        University of Winnipeg
        515 Portage Avenue
        Winnipeg, Man. R3B 2E9
        (204) 786-7811
     Hours: 9-4 M-F.
     Access: By appointment.
     Copying facilities.
Sources:
DCRMR (Records of Manitoba Conference of Methodist Church,
the United Church, & of the Presbyterian Synod; papers of
John McKay, George Brice, John King, & Andrew Baird).
Published finding aids: Directory of Archives in Manitoba
(Winnipeg, n.d.).

NEW BRUNSWICK

359. ANGLICAN CHURCH OF CANADA ARCHIVES
        Diocese of Fredricton
        808 Brunswick Street
        Fredericton, N.B. E3B 1J1
        (506) 454-4821
     Hours: By appointment only.
     Access: Reference only.
     Copying facilities.
Sources:
DCRMR (Parish records & registers; synod records).
Published finding aids: None.

360 .   PROVINCIAL ARCHIVES OF NEW BRUNSWICK
             P.O. Box 6000
             Fredericton, N.B. E3B 5H1
             (506) 453-2122
         Hours: 8:30-5 M-Sat.
         Access: Open.
         Copying facilities.
Sources:
Government records; including Customs House-Passenger Lists,
1833-37 (10,000 names; most from England & Ireland); land
petitions, 1783-1850 (25,000 names; nominal index); Naturalization of Aliens Administration Records, 1785-1867 (mostly
Americans who became British citizens; 1,000 names indexed);
Records of Immigration Administration, 1785-1867, and 1851
census; private collections include John Mann Papers, c. 1823
-32; James Brown Papers, 1813-16, 1838-62; Robert Eady Letters
1826-38; and Morrell Family Papers, 1828-1919.
Published finding aids: None.

NEWFOUNDLAND

361 .   MARITIME HISTORY GROUP
             c/o Department of History
             Memorial University of Newfound
             St. Johns, NF. A1B 3Y1
             (709) 753-1200
         Hours: 9-5 M-F.
         Access: By permission.
         Copying facilities.
Sources:
DCRMR (English, Irish, Scots, & Newfoundland genealogical
material; records relating to history of shipping, fishing,
and trade).
Published finding aids: None.

362 .   NEWFOUNDLAND HISTORICAL SOCIETY
             c/o Provincial Reference Library
             Arts & Culture Centre
             Allandale Road
             St. Johns, NF. A1B 3A3
             (709) 753-2781
         Hours: 10-9:30 M-Th.
                10-8:30 F.
                10-5:30 Sat. (Sept. 15-June 15).
         Access: Query first.
         Copying facilities.
Sources:
DCRMR (Private papers, newspapers, and maps pertaining to
the province).
Published finding aids: None.

363.   PROVINCIAL ARCHIVES OF NEWFOUNDLAND & LABRADOR
          Colonial Building, Military Road
          St. Johns, NF. A1C 2C9
          (709) 753-9380/ 9390/ 9398
       Hours: 9-5 M-F.
          & 6:30-9:45 p.m. W-Th.
       Access: Most records are open to the public.
       Copying facilities.
Sources:
Colonial & government records of Newfoundland, parish re-
cords, records of vital statistics, court records, street
directories, voters lists, many private & public collections;
NO family histories.
Published finding aids: None.

364.   TRINITY HISTORICAL SOCIETY
          Trinity, T.B., NF. A0C 2S0
          (709) 464-3657
       Hours: By appointment only.
       Access: By appointment only.
       NO copying facilities.
Sources:
MS collections include "History of Early Business Firms in
Trinity"; "History of Trinity"; "Family Names of Newfoundland
& Labrador"; commercial records, court, church, shipping,
military, & disaster records; early maps, charts, plans,
diaries, and letters.
Published finding aids: None.

NOVA SCOTIA

365.   LOUISBOURG ARCHIVES
          Fortress of Louisbourg National Park, NS B0A 1M0
          (902) 733-2280
       Hours: 8-4:30 M-F.
       Access: Open.
       Copying facilities.
Sources:
DCRMR (Documents, diaries, & maps relating to history of
Louisbourg & Cape Breton Island, 16th-19th centuries).
Published finding aids: None.

366.   ANGLICAN CHURCH OF CANADA ARCHIVES
          Diocese of Nova Scotia
          5732 College Street
          Halifax, NS   B3H 1X3
          (902) 423-8301
       Hours/Access: By appointment only.
       Copying facilities.
Sources:
DCRMR (Parish records & registers of the Diocese).
Published finding aids: None.

367 . PUBLIC ARCHIVES OF NOVA SCOTIA
            6016 University Avenue
            Halifax, NS   B3H 1W4
            (902) 423-9115
        Hours: 8:30-10 M-F.
               9-6   Sat.
               1-10   Sun.
        Access: Open.
        Copying facilities.
Sources:
Vital statistics, church registers, township registers,
census records, Land Papers, probate court records, Loyalist
Claims, immigration & passenger lists, newspapers. Printed
materials dealing with the four groups of this directory.
Published finding aids: Julie Morris, Tracing Your Ancesters
in Nova Scotia (PANS, 1981, 2nd ed.), and others.

368 . UNITED CHURCH OF CANADA
            Maritime Conference Archives
            Pine Hill Divinity Hall
            Francklyn Street
            Halifax, NS   B3H 3B5
            (902) 429-4819
        Hours: 9-12 M-F.
        Access: Open.
        Copying facilities.
Sources:
DCRMR (Records of United Church, Maritime Conference, & Con-
gregationalist, Methodist, & Presbyterian Churches before
1925, including Bermuda Methodists).
Published finding aids: None.

369 . CENTRE ACADIEN
            College Sainte-Anne
            Church Point, Nouvelle-Ecosse, NS   BOW 1M0
            (902) 769-2114
        Hours: 9-5 M & W.
        Access: By appointment only.
        Copying facilities.
Sources:
DCRMR (Private archives of maps, genealogies, pictures,
journals, & other documents relating to the Acadiens of
Nouvelle-Ecosse, Prince Edward Island, & New Brunswick).
Published finding aids: None.

ONTARIO

370 . YORK UNIVERSITY ARCHIVES
            105 Scott Library
            4700 Keele Street
            Downsview, Ont.   M3J 2R2
            (416) 667-3306

Hours: 8:30-4:30 M-F.
Access: Some collections restricted.
Sources:
Gilchrist Family Receipts, 1885-1912 & Genealogy of Henry
McCuaig, 1797-1881, and his wife Janet Colder, 1799-1872;
Alexander Ross Family Correspondence, 1810-1903; Schreiber
Family & Pedigree, 1680-1960; Sibbald Family Papers, 1771-
1914 (letters, diaries, journals, deeds, etc.); Frank W.
Wiggins Typescripts of The Immigrant, An Autobiography.
Published finding aids: York University Archives Accession
Bulletin No. 6, Sept., 1982.

371. QUEEN'S UNIVERSITY ARCHIVES
        Kathleen Ryan Hall
        Kingston, Ont. K7L 5C4
        (613) 547-3226
      Hours: 9-12 & 1-5 M-F.
        (Summer: 8:30-12 & 1-4:30).
      Access: Open.
      Copying facilities.
Sources:
Archives of the city of Kingston, archives of the university,
business collections, regional collections, literary collections, family papers & other manuscripts. Check for all four
groups of this directory.
Published finding aids: Anne McDermain, A Guide to the Holdings of Queen's University Archives (Kingston: QU, 1978).

372. PUBLIC ARCHIVES OF CANADA
        395 Wellington Street
        Ottawa, Ont. K1A 0N3
        (613) 992-2669
      Hours: 8:30-4:45 M-F.
      Access: Most collections open.
      Copying facilities.
Sources:
This Canadian equivalent of the American National Archives
in D.C. has many important immigration-related collections.
Federal Archives Division has several record groups related
to the topic. Immigration Branch (passenger manifests for
Canadian & some American cities, 1865-1908); British Archives
Section includes Colonial Office Records and Treasury Records.
Private collections include numerous diaries, family histor-
ies, letters, local histories, and church histories; also,
papers of individuals who organized colonies (e.g., Lord
Selkirk & Peter Robinson) and records of Colonial organiza-
tions (e.g., British American Land Company, British Dominions
Emigration Society, & Society for the Overseas Settlement of
British Women); much more.
Published finding aids: T. Cook & G.T. Wright, Federal Archives Division (PA, 1983); General Inventory: Manuscripts,
vols. 1-5, 7-8 (1972-77); others in preparation.

373. ARCHIVES OF ONTARIO
            77 Grenville Street
            Toronto, Ont. M7A 2R9
            (416) 965-5317
       Hours: 8:15-10:30 M-F.
               10-8 Sat. (By permission).
       Access: Open.
       Copying facilities.
Sources:
Government papers including Crown Land Papers, 1780-1915;
census & assessment rolls (8 counties), 1800-ca. 1870;
assessment rolls of Southern Ontario, 1850-1900; probate &
surrogate court records, 1793-1943. Private papers with focus
on genealogy and family data, includes Perkins Bull Collection (Peel County region), F.E. Macdonald Papers & F.D. Mc-
Lennan Collection (Glengarry County), & Peter Robinson Papers
(Peterborough region).
Published finding aids: Inventories of government records &
computerized Lands Records Index.

374. PRESBYTERIAN CHURCH IN CANADA ARCHIVES
            59 St. George Street
            Toronto, Ont. M5S 2EG
            (416) 595-1277
       Hours: 8:30-12:15 & 1:15-4:30 M-F.
       Access: Phone before visiting; some materials are re-
               stricted.
       Copying facilities.
Sources:
Church registers from throughout the country; church & some
family histories, head office records (minutes, reports, &
correspondence), mission records post 1925, personal papers,
scrapbooks, periodicals re. Presbyterian Church in Canada.
(See also, United Church Archives, Victoria University, for
pre-1925 materials).
Published finding aids: Union List of Manuscripts in Canadian
Repositories (Ottawa, 1975) & Supplements (1976, 1978, 1980).

375. UNITED CHURCH OF CANADA CENTRAL ARCHIVES
            Victoria University
            Toronto, Ont. M5S 2C4
            (416) 978-3832
       Hours: 9-5 M-F.
       Access: By permission.
       Copying facilities.
Sources:
DCRMR (Records of the United Church & its predecessors -
Methodist, Presbyterian, Congregational, Evangelical, &
United Brethren; registers of local churches in Southern
Ontario).
Published finding aids: Union List of Manuscripts in Canadian
Repositories (Ottawa, 1975) & Supplements (1976, 1978, 1980).

376 . UNIVERSITY OF TORONTO LIBRARY, SPECIAL COLLECTIONS
         120 St. George Street
         Toronto, Ont. M5S 1A5
         (416) 978-5285
         Hours: 9-5 M-Sat. (Oct.-Apr.).
                9-5 M-F. (May-Sept.).
         Access: By permission.
         Copying facilities.
Sources:
DCRMR (Documents relating to Canadian exploration & history;
records of Canadian business and other organizations).
Published finding aids: Union List of Manuscripts in Canadian
Repositories (Ottawa, 1975) & Supplements (1976, 1978, 1980).

PRINCE EDWARD ISLAND

377. PRINCE EDWARD ISLAND HERITAGE FOUNDATION
         2 Kent Street/ P.O. Box 902
         Charlottetown, PEI C1A 7L9
         (902) 892-9127
         Hours: 9-5 M-F & 7-9 p.m. Th.
         Access: By permission.
         Copying facilities.
Sources:
DCRMR (Genealogical material, business papers, diaries, maps,
minutebooks).
Published finding aids: None.

378. PUBLIC ARCHIVES OF PRINCE EDWARD ISLAND
         P.O. Box 7000
         Charlottetown, PEI C1A 7M4
         (902) 892-3504
         Hours: 8:30-5 M-F.
         Access: Some government documents restricted.
         Copying facilities.
Sources:
Government records, including Customs & Public Lands; corpor-
ate records, including Matthew & MacLean, 1870-1945, and
United Church, Cornwall, Parish records, 1856-1945; private
ms, including Palmer Family Papers, 1820-1918; the Port Hill
Papers, 1820-1918; and the diaries of Dr. John MacKieson;
newspapers from 1787, maps from the 1760's.
Published finding aids: None.

QUEBEC

(The province of Quebec has preserved mostly archives relating to the French, especially genealogy. The user of this
directory should, therefore, consult the Public Archives of
Canada in Ottawa, as well as the repositories listed below).

379 .   CANADIAN PACIFIC RAILWAY COMPANY
                Windsor Station
                Montreal, QU. H3C 3E4
                (514) 861-6811
        Hours/Access: By written permission.
Sources:
DCRMR (Financial records, correspondence, personal papers,
& reports).
Published finding aids: None.

380 .   MCGILL UNIVERSITY ARCHIVES
                McLennan Library
                3459 McTarish Street/ P.O. Box 6070, Station A
                Montreal, QU. H3A 1Y1
                (514) 392-5356
        Hours: 9-12:30 & 1:30-5 M-F.
        Access: Most collections open.
        Copying facilities.
Sources:
Sir William Dawson & Family Records, 1820-1899; United Church
of Canada - Montreal/Ottawa Conference Papers, c. 1820-1960;
Montreal General Hospital Records, 1820-1980; Royal Hospital
Records, 1889-1980; McGill University Administrative Records.
Published finding aids: General guide only.

381 .   SOCIETE D'HISTOIRE DES CANTONS DE L'EST (Archives)
                Howardene, C.P. 1141
                Sherbrooke, QU. J1H 2T6
                (819) 526-0616
        Hours: 9:30-12 & 2-5 M-Th.
               2-5 & 7:45-10 F.
        Access: Open.
        NO copying facilities.
Sources:
DCRMR (Regional & personal papers, maps, and pictures from
1810-1930).
Published finding aids: None.

382 .   ARCHIVES NATIONALES DU QUEBEC
                Parc des Champs-de-fataille
                Quebec, QU. G1A 1A3
                (418) 643-2167
        Hours: 8:30-4:30 M-F.
        Access: Open.
        NO copying facilities.
Sources:
DCRMR (Materials, from 1609, include government records,

maps, diaries, genealogies, and microfilm copies of records
in other repositories).
Published finding aids: Inventories of the collections.

383 . MONASTÈRE DES AUGUSTINES DE L'HÔPITOL-GÉNÉRAL
        260 Boulevard Langelier
        Quebec, QU. G1K 5N1
        (418) 524-2115
        Hours/Access: By appointment only.
        NO copying facilities.
Sources:
DCRMR (Hospital records from 1645-1976).
Published finding aids: None.

SASKATCHEWAN

384 . LUTHERAN CHURCH - MISSOURI SYNOD
        Archives of the Manitoba-Saskatchewan District
        1927 Grant Drive
        Regina, SaS. S4S 4V6
        (306) 378-6095
        Hours: 9-5 M-F.
        Access: Open.
        Copying facilities.
Sources:
DCRMR (Records of baptisms, marriages, and deaths; synod
records; autobiographies of early pastors; old Bible & hymn-
books).
Published finding aids: None.

385 . SASKATCHEWAN ARCHIVES BOARD, REGINA OFFICE
        University of Regina
        Regina, SaS. S4S 0A2
        (306) 565-4067
        Hours: 8:30-5 M-F. & by appointment.
        Access: Open.
        Copying facilities.
Sources:
Dept. of Education, school district files; Homestead Records;
Petitions, 1888-1944; local histories (many), maps, news-
papers & periodicals; St. Andrews Colony Collection (Scottish);
"The Irish Colony, 1905-1955"; Welsh Presbyterian Church at
Bangor Correspondence; St. David's Society of Regina Records,
1940-73; George H. Morris Papers, 1865-1965; more.
Published finding aids: Guides & Inventories to most collec-
tions.

386 . LUTHERAN CHURCH IN AMERICA
        Archives of Central Canada Synod
        c/o Lutheran Theological Seminary
        Saskatoon, SaS. S7N 0X3
        (306) 343-6897

Hours/Access: By appointment only.
Copying facilities.
Sources:
DCRMR (Records & ms relating to the synod and its predeces-
sors, their sub-groups and congregations).
Published finding aids: None.

387 . SASKATCHEWAN PUBLIC LIBRARY
              23rd Street & 4th Avenue
              Saskatchewan, SaS. S7K 0J6
              (306) 652-7313
        Hours: 1:30-5 M-Sat.
        Access: Open.
        Copying facilities.
Sources:
DCRMR (Newspapers, ethnic material, Northwest Rebellion
items, items related to the fur trade, reference materials
for Saskatchewan).
Published finding aids: None.

388 . UNITED CHURCH OF CANADA, SASKATCHEWAN CONFERENCE
              St. Andrew's College
              University of Saskatchewan
              Saskatchewan, SaS. S7N 0W3
              (306) 343-5146
        Hours/Access: By appointment only.
        Copying facilities.
Sources:
DCRMR (Records of the Presbyterian Synod, Methodist Church
Conference, The United Church, and parish records for this
province).
Published finding aids: None.

YUKON TERRITORY

389.   YUKON ARCHIVES
              Box 2703
              Whitehorse, YT. Y1A 2C6
              (403) 667-5321
        Hours: 8:30-5 M-F. & by appointment.
        Access: Open.
        Copying facilities.
Sources:
DCRMR (Territorial government records, business records,
private papers, maps, newspapers).
Published finding aids: None.

INDEX

(References are to entry, not page numbers)

About the Compilers

JACK WAYNE WEAVER is Professor of English at Winthrop College, Rock Hill, South Carolina. He is the author of *Selected Proceedings of the Scotch-Irish Heritage Festival at Winthrop College*, *An Annotated Bibliography of Writings About Arthur Wing Pinero*, and articles in *English Literature in Translation*, *Appalachian Heritage*, and the *Journal of Irish Literature*.

DEEGEE LESTER previously worked as a sportswriter and Assistant to the Women's Sports Information Director at the University of Tennessee. She is the author of *Irish Research: A Guide to Collections in North America, Ireland, and Great Britain* (Greenwood Press, forthcoming).